American Queen

Farzana Moon

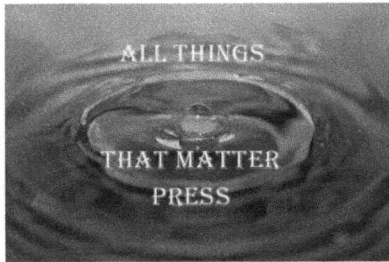
ALL THINGS
THAT MATTER
PRESS

American Queen

ISBN 13: 9781732723795

Library of Congress Control Number: 2019945548

Cover Photos: Supplied by Qahira Wirgman

Cover design © by All Things That Matter Press
Published in 2019 by All Things That Matter Press

This work is based upon true events; however, some events and conversations have been fictionalized to add to the telling of the story.

The American Queen is dedicated to Pir Zia the grandson of Ora Ray Baker and Hazrat Inayat Khan

Acknowledgement

Special thanks to Jennifer Alia Wittman for her time and kindness to lead me in the right direction to obtain photos of the family of Hazrat Inayat Khan and Ora Ray Baker. Also, a million thanks and profound gratitude to Qahira Wirgman for sending me all the photos for this book, American Queen. Greatly indebted to Nekbakht Foundation for helping me out with photos and encouragement.

Prologue

American Queen ~ Ora Ray Baker

O Beloved, is my love so weak
That it bringeth me not to Thee
Then let me weep more and more each day
Till by weeping, it strengthened be
But when its strength be still too less
And the fountain of tears run dry
Tears of blood, let me weep, yea until
By weeping for Thee, I may die
~Pirani

Ora Ray Baker, who was fated to fall in love with an Indian Mystic, not only became the Queen of Hazrat Inayat Khan's heart, but the Queen of fortitude, devotion and endurance, if not a saint, suffering countless tragedies and yet persevering. She finally succumbed to death a few years after WW II when she discovered that her daughter was killed by the Nazis in the concentration camps.

Disregarding the discrepancies in Ora Ray Baker's birth year and birthplace, she was presumably born May 8, 1892 in Kansas or in Albuquerque, New Mexico, the latter place most favored by the researchers. She herself wrote that her mother's maiden name was Wyatt. Later she named her mother Margaret Hiatt, nicknamed Aletta whose father was born in Indiana. Her mother Aletta came from Maryland — home of many Kemp family members. Aletta had a twin sister named Alice. Ora Ray Baker started writing poetry as a young girl and continued that practice on and off whenever inspired to express her joy or grief.

Conflicting reports of researchers show that the Kemp family came from Bavaria. One report reveals that throughout several generations between Johann Conrad Kaempff, Kemp, and Mary May Kemp, Ora Ray's maternal grandmother, came from Germany or Switzerland. So, Ora Ray's heritage consisted of Swiss or German.

Erastus Warren Baker show him to have been born in 1850 in Kentucky and his wife in Iowa. On Ora Ray's marriage certificate in 1913 she wrote her father was a lawyer. Ora Ray had a stepbrother from her father's first marriage and when her own mother left her father, she was raised by her stepbrother, Pierre Bernard, a yoga teacher and a great musician.

Against the wishes of her stepbrother she married Hazrat Inayat Khan. Endowed with poetic spirit and always hungering for the crumbs of spirituality, she rejected the conventional style of marriage in America which her brother wanted — her to be a part of elite and wealthy circle of friends. Instead, she chose the life of mystery and mysticism with her mystic husband, traveling in Europe and experiencing profound joy of love in marriage along with the profundity of music and Sufi teaching of her mystic husband. It was the power of this love which made her withstand hosts of tragedies after the untimely death of Hazrat Inayat Khan.

Ora Ray Baker was titled Amina Begum after her marriage. She was Hazrat Inayat Khan's Sharda, meaning goddess. He also bestowed upon her the title of Pirani-PiRani, meaning queen of Pir—spiritual guide and teacher.

The way of illumination
Is the path that leads to God
May ye seek that revelation
Forever this pathway trod
And behold the light eternal
When the end is drawing nigh
Its rays spread forth upon ye all
As a crown to glorify
~Pirani

Child of Light

A little fairy told me why the flowers wake in May
She said it's for the Birthday of a little Ora Ray
The Sun, they say, is jealous of her lovely golden hair
The flowers, look their sweetest, just try to be as fair
~Noor

If God was the king within Hazrat Inayat Khan's heart, then Ora Ray became the Queen inside the sacred shrine of his heart, but that's his love story. Her life story begins in Albuquerque, New Mexico. She was born on May 8, 1892, her name Ora Ray meaning literally, aura of light rays. She was the youngest of the three sisters, Allie May, Lula Fay and Lela Murley, and one brother named Earl. Ora Ray had another older sibling, a half-brother, Pierre Bernard, from her father's previous marriage to his distant cousin Catherine Givens. Originally, he was named Peter, but later when his mother married John C. Bernard, allegedly related to a famous French psychologist by the name of Claude Bernard, he changed his name. Claude Bernard was also famous for his scientific research in medicine. Considering his stepfather's fame, Peter Baker changed his name to Pierre Bernard.

According to the popular consensus of the researchers, Ora Ray's mother's name was Margaret Hiatt from a prosperous family by the name of Kemp from Switzerland, who later immigrated to Pennsylvania. Ora Ray's father's name was Eurastus Warren Baker who owned a family farm. He studied to be a lawyer, then became the editor of his own newspaper, owing to his love for arts and literature. Musically inclined, he composed a song named, Old Rose. He also owned the Baker Wire Company in Illinois.

Ora Ray grew up in a wealthy home with all the comforts any child would ever desire. She was frail and beautiful. Her reason for frail health was that she had contracted typhoid fever in her early childhood. The family doctor had expressed little hope of her survival after the fever, but even at that tender age between childhood and teens, she insisted that she would live her dream of music and literature. Persevering against all odds, by the virtue of her own faith and courage, she was restored to good health. As Ora Ray gained swift, miraculous recovery, her doctor was astonished beyond belief. Later ascribing the miracle of her good health to her own willpower as a young girl, so very mature above the pale of her tender years.

Though blessed with luxurious living and surrounded by abundance and affluence, sadness visited Ora Ray early in life since her parents' relationship proved to be aloof and uncongenial. She was more attached to her father, so she chose to stay with him when the parents separated. Her father was more attentive to her upbringing, keen and observant of her sadness and sensitivity. He would tell her stories of his famous ancestors. Touched with tenderness, he rewarded his daughter most generously whatever her little heart desired since Ora Ray was always attentive, sitting there rapt, listening to his stories, and at times bursting with interest and enthusiasm.

Noteworthy amongst the patrimony were her grandfather Judge S. Baker who became a senator in Albuquerque, New Mexico. Another wealthy member of the family was George W. Baker who was raised in Iowa and managed a cattle ranch in New Mexico's Cimarron Valley. A female cousin of Ora Ray's mother was another distinguished member of the Baker family. Her name was Mary Baker Eddy, the founder of the Christian Science Movement.

Growing up as a young lady, Ora Ray was drawn to the beauty of nature and loved excursions. During the vacations from school, her father would take her on train trips to enjoy the pristine vastness of the countryside. They would travel in private compartments, very comfortable and beautifully furnished. The dining cars were spacious with formal settings of silver on white linen tablecloths. Ora Ray admired the lovely floral arrangements on the tables as well as the scenic splendor of the countryside.

Nostalgic memories of such trips would stay with Ora Ray for the rest of her life as she would reminisce with great fondness of the fabulous times she had spent with her father. She was impressed by the few skyscrapers she had seen in New York, lofty and soaring. Amongst her favorite sites was the Statue of Liberty, so very grand, imposing, and all-encompassing. In her diary she wrote she was in awe the first time her eyes settled on the façade of the Empire State Building. She was overwhelmed by the teeming crowds on the Fifth Avenue, 42nd street and the East River. Great Hudson River with its glittering waves she loved, often lingering there to watch the sunsets that were so tranquil and heliotrope. Her bewilderment was great when she first saw the city of Manhattan lit to brilliance in the evening supplied by the power lines of electricity invented by Thomas Alva Edison. Leaning against her father she stood in awe, unable to comprehend how light can transform the entire city to such vibrant pulse of life and laughter.

During one of those trips with her father, Ora Ray met her half-brother Pierre Bernard. He was seventeen years older than her and already well established as a yoga teacher in New York. Pierre professed to be an authority on yoga along with the mastery of Sanskrit language. He was prone to boast that he studied for years in India under the tutelage of a Sanskrit scholar. Ora Ray, though young and perceptive, was greatly impressed by him when he told her that he was the first American to introduce the philosophy and the practices of yoga and Tantra to American aspirants. Pierre was kind and indulgent with Ora Ray, taking her to the New York Sanskrit College Library. Looking at the gleaming shelves brimming with Sanskrit books, Ora Ray was lured toward Pierre like a magnet toward a steel of knowledge. Poet at heart and in temperament, she looked up to him as a mentor, if not an odd sibling worthy of reverence.

With the passing of time Ora Ray had blossomed to be a lady of immense courage and longed to explore the world. Her father, noticing his daughter's enthusiasm, presented her with a unique set of gifts upon her graduation. Ora Ray received twenty-five traveling trunks, each containing a full wardrobe with matching accessories, also gold coins and dollar bills stuffed in her new purses. Overwhelmed with gratitude and taking advantage of these generous gifts, Ora Ray chose as her base the home of her half-brother Pierre in Lonia, New Jersey. She traveled extensively. She went to Kansas to see her grandmother, then explored the cities of Seattle and San Francisco.

While Ora Ray was away from home, her mother passed away. Ora Ray's father's health was also declining after the death of his already estranged wife. So, he made Pierre Ora Ray's legal guardian after Pierre got married to a French girl by the name of Blanche De Viers. Soon after her stay with Pierre, tragic news reached her that her father, too, passed away. Innately spiritual and contemplative, Ora Ray learnt yoga and meditation from Pierre and lived harmoniously with him and his wife. She was not to stay with them for long, for soon the arrow of cupid would strike her heart, transporting her from the rich soil of America into arms of her beloved in lands that were distant and tumultuous.

***

Yoga and meditation had helped Ora Ray to cope with the loss of her parents, but some sort of void had settled in her heart. Solitude and loneliness were her best of friends and she had renewed her habit of writing poetry.

> Come, little birds at my window
> And feed from out of my hand
> My envy oft to you doth go
> Soaring over sea and land
> No pain to bear, nor care, nor woe
> No chain to bind you tight
> Flying cheerfully to and fro
> In happy, playful flight
> But then again methinks it less
> Than happiness I gain
> While this poor heart is in distress
> Wrapped in grief and pain

One night she dreamed that a sage—an eastern mystic came to her. He lifted her into his arms, and both soared above the seas and aimed for the heavens painted with the rainbows. Awakening from that deep slumber as she called it, she felt exultant beyond expression. Now she was experiencing another dream in her waking state that she would become the queen of the heavens and the earth and would embrace willingly both love and grief and would get to know both fortunes and tragedies.

Ora Ray's dreams were becoming her constant companions in her waking and sleeping hours. Sometimes she was transported into lands alien, engulfed in fogs of danger, a completely strange world of illusions, cruelties and destruction. Most of her dreams were serene, revealing glimpses of her mystic sage-prince who would love her as no other woman on earth had ever been loved before. In her dreams she experienced the pure bliss of love, but then pincers of grief would envelop her, holding her prisoner in torments indescribable.

Another time, in another world, a mystic prince was being forged out of a royal lineage to enchant Ora Ray with his love. Paradoxically, the mystic she envisioned in her dreams so often would materialize. She would meet him face to face, longing to fly into his arms to be carried to heights unattainable.

Each morn I see the sun in majesty
Come back to shine as thy rival as before
But O what ages has it taken thee
To come home—if thou wilt come, once more
~Arzu

Endowed with a poetic spirit, Ora Ray had matured into a young lady of such profound courage that she could rise above any adversity even to challenge fate if it threatened her sense of freedom. Part of her strength and determination was the result of her daily discipline in mediation. She had learned the art of deep contemplation from Pierre and had grown fond of her brother and his wife. Though, she had begun to feel that history was repeating itself for she could see the life-pattern of her deceased parents. Rarely did she see her brother and his wife together. Pierre was mostly on tours, teaching yoga, or giving lectures. His wife had her own circle of friends, though she, too, was away from home quite often, spending more time in the home of her parents.

Ora Ray had great respect for her brother and looked up to him as her spiritual guide and guardian. Pierre, in return, was rather possessive of Ora Ray as his little sister, attentive to her needs and indulgent to all her whims with the generosity of a wealthy ward. Under his guidance she studied literature, also learning the theory of music. She had taken courses in journalism and was actively in touch with her distant cousin Mary Baker Eddy, the founder of the Christian Science Magazine.

Dubbed as a travel queen by her friends, Ora Ray visited many states in America. Occasionally, she accompanied Pierre on his business trips to San Francisco with the hope of seeing her cousin Mary Baker Eddy whom she held in high regard, praising Mary as being spiritually advanced and delightfully intelligent. It was during one of those visits to San Francisco that Pierre took her to attend a lecture and a concert at the Ramakrishna Ashram.

The Ashram was teeming with an enthusiastic crowd, a motley group of young and old, talking about the Royal Musicians of India who had attained fame as to charming the audience to awe and rapture with their music. Ora Ray could feel the pulse of excitement in this vast hall, rippling in wave upon wave of joyful anticipation. Before she knew, this spirit of collective joy was infused inside her own soul and psyche, as if something miraculous was going to transform her whole being into the light of love.

Seated beside Pierre and watching the stage lights being switched on, Ora Ray was transported into a world beyond her wildest of imaginations. The lead musician, Hazrat Inayat Khan, was being introduced as a Sufi, an accomplished singer, and a spiritual teacher. She sat spellbound, unable to tear her gaze away from the resinous glow of sunshine in his eyes, his tall figure radiating glow and magnetism. The large ruby in his turban against the shaft of light throbbed like a fresh wound carved right out of her own heart. She sat glued to her seat, rapt and smitten.

The musicians had begun to tune their instruments, and she was becoming aware of the abrupt thundering of her heart as if it was going to explode out of her body and perish into some ethereal and boundless realm.

The Ashram was plunged in utter silence as soon as Hazrat Inayat Khan began teasing the strings of his veena. His cousin and brothers were accompanying him on tablas, trumpet, and trombone. How long did they play, Ora Ray had no idea. All she knew was that her heart danced amidst clouds of musical notes. Those fiery notes were alive, rippling, spiraling and all-encompassing before expanding into firework. Living. Whirling in some mad dance of life and death, expiring inside their own accolade of exaltation.

A sudden thundering of applause shook the hall. Ora Ray was jolted out of her dream reveries. Hazrat Inayat Khan, being the key speaker, rose to his feet and began his discourse. The sonorous notes in his own expression enveloped the audience once again in waters of perfect stillness. He was talking about love, Sufism and God Realization. Ora Ray sat there half swooning, half listening, yet drinking deep draughts of sweetness from the richness in his voice, her heart thundering again, leaping and somersaulting.

At the end of the brief discourse by Hazrat Inayat Khan, Ora Ray's trance, this second time around, was broken by another round of thunderous applause. Pierre, well established in literary circles, in addition to being a member of elite group and having had the chance to meet Hazrat Inayat Khan a few times before in New York, took this opportunity to introduce his sister to the accomplished Indian Mystic and Musician.

With the possessiveness of a doting father, Pierre clutched Ora Ray's small hand into his firm grip and escorted her behind the stage where the musicians sat talking and laughing. He introduced Ora Ray as his little sister, singling out Hazrat Inayat Khan as the one worthy of introduction. One look at the angelic face of Ora Ray, sparkling blue eyes and golden hair, Hazrat Inayat Khan's heart lurched, but master of his emotions always, he bowed and smiled. Their eyes met and the arrow of cupid pierced their hearts. Whose heart bled the most, only the lovers would be able to confess later to each other amidst their fears of separation or longings for nearness.

If Hazrat Inayat Khan was the master of his emotions, Ora Ray proved to be the mistress of her own anguished heart, only smiling in return. Something ineffable had haloed both Ora Ray and Hazrat Inayat

Khan in the mysterious lights of love, brilliant little sparks of bliss in the promise of union inside the very silence of their hearts.

Pierre didn't notice any mysterious connection between his sister and the Mystic, so impressed he was by his musical talent that he was requesting Hazrat Inayat Khan if he would be willing to give veena lessons to his sister. Hazrat Inayat Khan replied most gallantly that it would be his pleasure entirely to teach Ora Ray the melodious notes of music on veena.

After this gracious response, Pierre was distracted by one of his rich friends who had followed him, most anxious to know if he, Pierre, would join him at the buffet table. Meanwhile, Hazrat Inayat Khan's cousin and brothers were also leaving to enjoy the Indian-style buffet prepared in honor of the musicians. Pierre agreed to join his friend, allowing his sister to converse with the great musician, though commenting over his shoulders before leaving that he would be waiting for them soon in the dining hall.

Finding themselves alone, both Ora Ray and Hazrat Inayat Khan seemed suspended in abeyance. Ora Ray was the first one to summon enough courage to request if he would, in the near future, grant her an interview which she wished to send to the newspaper for publication. Hazrat Inayat Khan, beaming with love and gratitude, heaved a sigh of relief, exclaiming, "Now is a good time as any. Please stay. To refresh my own memory is a feast I get to enjoy occasionally."

As if enveloped in the warmth of a subtle bliss—almost a sweet caress, Ora Ray spurted forth her first question. Paradoxically, a precursor to countless more, never reaching the bottomless depths of a mysterious ocean.

"Why is your group called the Royal Musicians of India?" Ora Ray asked

"You have touched the tender strings of past pride too heavy for my weak shoulders, my Sharda, if I may be as bold as to address you in such a manner." Hazrat Inayat Khan began wistfully, his tone both respectful and endearing. Since Ora Ray only smiled her assent, he continued. "Sharda meaning goddess in our language. Back to the past pride—this false pride becomes a means of subsistence in this material world where exotic names attract audience for the benefit of sharing a noble message, in addition to earning an honest living."

Hazrat Inayat Khan's gentle tones, brimming with love profound on the verge of sadness, had lulled Ora Ray to a sense of deep serenity. She sat in rapt wonder, utterly absorbed in taking mental notes.

"Each child can claim the title of royalty if it can trace its lineage back to Adam." Hazrat Inayat Khan smiled and resumed, sensing her avid curiosity. "In my case, I am the descendant of King Tipu Sultan of India. My maternal grandmother was a descendant of the ruler of Mysore. Tipu Sultan was married to my grandmother. He was called the Tiger of Mysore who resisted intrusion of the British East India Company, but was finally killed on a battlefield in Year 1799 while defending his kingdom of Mysore. Tipu Sultan himself was the descendant of the Moghul emperors, who, after the collapse of the Moghul Empire, still held on to his remnant of a kingdom until he was defeated and killed by the British. My grandfather Maula Bakhsh married one of Tipu Sultan's granddaughters. One of Maula Bakhsh's daughters married Rahmat Khan who became my father. He came from the lineage of Chishti Order of the Sufis. Sufis are usually Muslim saints who rise to that status when they attain the mastery of God Realization. I was born into a musical family as well as the spiritual one in the city of Baroda July 5, 1882 in India. As far as I can remember, I have been spiritually inclined to study and explore all religions. In my youth I learned to play various music instruments from my grandfather, in my spare time, wandering in search of the saints and the mystics. I didn't know what I was searching for until I met a great Sufi teacher by the name of Abu Hashim Madani. He became my friend and spiritual guide, training me in the Way of four major Sufi Orders—Chishti, Qadiri, Suhrawardi, and Naqshabandi. Before his death my Murshid—meaning teacher, my Sufi teacher Madani instructed me: *Fare forth into the world, my child, and harmonize the East and the West with the harmony of thy music. Spread the wisdom of Sufism abroad, for to this end thou art gifted by Allah, the most Merciful and Compassionate.* In obedience to my Murshid I sailed from India to America September 13, 1910 and am still trying to balance the lyric and poetry of my motherland with this world of industry and commerce."

"What is Sufism?" Ora Ray could barely murmur. Her heart longing for his soothing inflections which she wanted to hear 'til eternity.

"Very simple, yet most difficult to explain, this Sufism." Hazrat Inayat Khan's own heart was singing paeans of love. "Briefly, Sufism strives towards bringing about in the world the realization of the divinity of human soul, which hitherto has been overlooked, for the reason that time had not come. The principle thing that the Sufi message has to accomplish in this era is to create the realization of the divine spark in every soul that every soul according to its progress may begin to realize itself the spark of divinity within. That is the task before us."

"What is this message?" Ora Ray queried. She was trying her best not to swoon against the dance of gold in his eyes, more poetic than his verbal expression.

"The message, my Sharda." Hazrat Inayat Khan began under some spell of ecstatic abandon. "Yes, the message that the whole humanity is as one single body and all nations and communities and races as the different organs for the happiness and wellbeing of whole body. If there is one organ of the body in pain, the whole body must sustain a share of the strain. By this message, mankind may begin to think that his welfare and his wellbeing is not in looking after himself, but it is in looking after others. All in all, when there will be love, goodness, reciprocity towards each other, the world would be a better place to live and enjoy."

"Are you succeeding in your mission—this message, in America, I mean?" Ora Ray was drawn to him like one moth to a flame, wishing this interview to be everlasting.

"If you call this success, giving public performances on Indian music!" Hazrat Inayat Khan's gold-brown eyes were a glow of sunshine. "More than a year has whirled past since I came here, and our music concerts have been successful by the grace of graceful dancers accompanying us, Mata Hari and Ruth St. Denis. Ruth is pleasantly witty. In response to my ideas about human brotherhood, uniting East and West, she quipped, 'We the people of Orient and Occident may be brothers, but not twins.' In addition to these musical concerts I have given Sufi lectures, my first one at the Columbia University in New York. Then in homes and bookstores. In San Francisco here I met a lady Mrs. Ada Martin, you will probably get to meet her soon. She became my first student in Sufism. It was swift and astonishing. When I was conversing with her, I noticed a rare phenomenon, the whole room seemed to be lit up with bright light. I am not sure if she noticed it, but the next day I was compelled to initiate her as a Sufi. She became my first mureed— meaning Sufi student, in America. As is tradition, I invested her with a new name, Rabia, in remembrance of an ancient woman saint of Basra in Iraq, who was known as the Sufi Mistress of the Sufi Masters since her wisdom and knowledge exceeded men's in that age and time. She served as Murshid for many men and women."

"Are you Murshid then?" Ora Ray asked. Her heart sinking at the paucity of her own questions.

"In my homeland they call me Pir-O-Murshid, meaning that I belong to the lineage of the Sufi Masters in Chishti Order." Hazrat Inayat Khan smiled. The sun-gold in his eyes catching and holding the shuddering of awe and despair in her beautiful eyes, so pure and sparkling.

"Would you accept me as your mureed?" Ora Ray didn't know what to say, her heart melting and weeping.

'I should be the one begging you if you would consider marrying me?" Hazrat Inayat Khan's lips were uttering what his heart was commanding. He had fallen utterly and ineffably in love as if his heart had seen this angelic face even before his eyes witnessed the purity of her youth. "But take your time, my Sharda, no need to answer as yet. Considering, I am a homeless, wandering man on a mission of divine unity for all. It would be a lonely life for a young girl like you with angelic face and brilliant eyes the envy of the clear blue skies. For I would be away from home for lengthy periods of time, giving lectures, concerts. Please take your time and make a wise decision," he pleaded as if trying to escape the decree of hopelessness.

"I already feel I am a part of you." Ora Ray's white features were washed by a crimson flush. "Should I call you, Murshid?"

'My Sharda, the happiest of devotees at your feet." Hazrat Inayat Khan's very breath was worshiping the queen of his heart seated before him, crowned with the glow of purity and innocence. "I will be your Daya, meaning compassion, since this word connotes perfect love in all its essence. In fact, you would be my angelic Daya in perfect compassion, forgiving all my faults with compassion." He couldn't say more, noticing the return of his cousin and brothers.

"Have compassion on your mind and body, Murshid, by nourishing it with food." The cousin of Hazrat Inayat Khan said, catching only his last word.

Hazrat Inayat Khan, beaming with joy, took this opportunity to introduce Ora Ray to his cousin Mohammad Ali, his elder brother Mahboob Khan and his younger brother Musharaf Khan. Adding, that he would be giving veena lessons to Miss Ora Ray.

"Be warned, Miss Ora Ray," Musharaf Khan cautioned. "You might be starved, for Murshid forgets about food or sleep when engrossed in playing music or teaching."

The cousin and the brothers burst out laughing without restraint, Ora Ray joining in while noticing the return of her own brother, all flustered.

"Here you are. I was looking all over for you," Pierre exclaimed, courteously acknowledging the presence of all musicians.

"I am sure you have seen Pierre before." Hazrat Inayat Khan was quick to introduce him to his cousin and brothers. "He is the famous yoga teacher in New York. And he is the brother of Miss Ora Ray."

"Pleased to meet you." Pierre shook hands with all, contriving an amiable smile, then turning his attention to Hazrat Inayat Khan. "When can you start the veena lessons for my sister?"

"Tomorrow, if that is not too long a wait," Hazrat Inayat Khan quipped.

"Perfect, if it is all right with Ora. And I can tell she is ready." Pierre offered his arm to his sister, said a hasty goodbye to all the musicians, and both the brother and sister vanished behind the curtains.

1912 ~ Music of Love

Before my work is over
You, my Lord, will right the wrong
Before you play your music
Will you let me sing my song
~Hazrat Inayat Khan

San Francisco had become Ora Ray's haven of joys since the past few months of her veena lessons from Hazrat Inayat Khan. She was quick to learn how to play veena, but the music of love which poured out of Hazrat Inayat Khan's heart was her bliss. Perceptive as she was, she could literally inhale the scent of his nearness as if it was some sort of elixir, sweet and intoxicating, making her heart giddy and restless. She could feel her heart soaring up to the skies, sailing in the clouds, and riding on the rainbows. Hazrat Inayat Khan in return, smitten by her beauty and youthful innocence of love, could not conceal his own purity of love reflected in his eyes, reverent and shining as he would watch her fingers tease the strings of veena in worshipful silence.

Pierre was busy giving yoga lessons and planning to build another Academy in San Francisco. Ora Ray had the luxury of freedom to attend Hazrat Inayat Khan's lectures, along with her veena music lessons in between, willingly sanctioned by her brother. At times Hazrat Inayat Khan would teach her about the spiritual practices in Sufism. Those were moments when she would return home late, but Pierre didn't seem to notice since he was totally immersed in his new project of opening another academy. Meanwhile and unbeknown to him, Ora Ray and Hazrat Inayat Khan were verbally and spiritually engaged to be married. Hazrat Inayat Khan was booked for concerts and lectures and hoping for a lull so that he would have time to request Ora Ray's hand in marriage from Pierre since he was her legal guardian. Ora Ray, in fact, didn't want him to approach her brother in this delicate matter until she could make sure that her brother would not oppose this marriage.

Weeks were merging into months and even this balmy evening after the music lessons, Hazrat Inayat Khan was tempted to broach the subject of marriage, but he decided to quell this temptation. Ora Ray was eager to learn more about Sufism and was talking joyfully. She was describing her chance meeting with his Sufi disciple—mureed Rabia Martin and how Rabia herself had narrated her first encounter with Hazrat Inayat Khan—her Murshid.

Ada Martin, a married woman in her mid-thirties, had attended an Indian music concert performed by Hazrat Inayat Khan and his brothers, the opening of which was staged by an American dancer by the name of Ruth St. Denis. Mrs. Martin had enjoyed watching the American dancer, but when Hazrat Inayat Khan started playing his veena she was transported to some blissful realms beyond imagination, though Hazrat Inayat Khan was not even aware of her presence in the audience. She was so deeply touched by the aura of his glowing personality that she didn't know why she was feeling so light, so bewildered, and she didn't know it would not be until she visited his concert again that she would be initiated as a Sufi. Even after the concert she seemed to be in a trance, reaching home under some spell of exaltation. During the waking, sleeping hours of the night she had fallen into a spiritual state of utmost serenity. This state had lasted for several days, even her husband couldn't help noticing and commenting.

Prophet Muhammad had visited Mrs. Martin in her dreams, filling her heart with the light of love and compassion. She was under some spell of dream-awakening, not knowing that she was still enveloped by the spiritual state, compelled by this inexplicable longing to attend the next concert of Hazrat Inayat Khan scheduled in another city quite far from her own hometown. Fortunately, her husband understood her spiritual need and decided to borrow money from his friends so that she could attend that longed-for concert. Noticing her seated there in the first row rapt and wide-eyed, Hazrat Inayat Khan knew that she was already the recipient of Grace on the path to spiritual unfoldment. After the concert, he invited Mrs. Martin on the stage and initiated her as a Sufi Disciple, wondering how he missed her presence in the previous concert.

Hazrat Inayat Khan was the only and most attentive of Ora Ray's audience until she finished expressing Rabia's own personal confessions. Then he began softly and endearingly. "I am not sure, my Sharda, if you saw Rabia's little daughter, she is adorable." Hazrat Inayat Khan smiled.

"Rabia is the most loving of mothers, besides being dedicated to the spiritual movement of Sufism."

The golden light of tenderness in Hazrat Inayat Khan's eyes was lulling Ora Ray to blissful silence, and she sat there as usual luxuriating in the sweet cadence of his inflections.

"Actually, it has been more than a year ago when Rabia Martin finished her forty days of spiritual training and I bestowed upon her the title of Murshida." Hazrat Inayat Khan resumed reminiscently. "That means she has earned the status of Sufi Teacher who can accept students as mureeds and train them in the spiritual practices of Sufism. When I came to America, I didn't know how I was going to live and even the idea of sharing the knowledge of Sufism seemed like a distant dream, but this dream is slowly materializing into great possibilities. In between my travels and lectures I have gained a few mureeds: Ralph Parish, Miss Genie Nawn, Mrs. Logan, Miss Collins, Mrs. Eldering, and Mrs. Morrison. Paradoxically, the path of Sufism was left behind while I struggled to find means to earn my living. Music proved to be my friend and my source of income, with the help of my cousin and brothers of course, as I discovered early during my stay in America. My first opportunity came when I made acquaintance of Mr. Edmund. He was very generous to invite us to a reception at his studio where we performed. Soon we were giving concerts in private halls and affluent homes to audiences both avid and charming. Good luck seemed to favor us when we met a prominent singer by the name of Emma Thursby. She arranged for us to perform at large gatherings. We gave concerts at the Columbia University, meeting another prominent person—the head of the music department at the same university. His name was Dr. Deebner and we became great friends. I should stop, these dull details are putting you to sleep," He murmured in quick apology.

"Please don't stop," Ora Ray replied. "You would be robbing me of the pleasure of getting closer to you by learning about your work and friends and mureeds."

"In that case I dare not stop lest I be guilty of displeasure." Hazrat Inayat Khan laughed, quick to reminisce once again. "It was at the Columbia University where I met Ruth St. Denis also, I told you about her witty remark already. She got interested in our Indian music, making it a part of her dancing routine. As our concerts gained popularity we started touring within the United States. I had a chance to speak to a very large audience at the University of Los Angeles and at the Berkley University here in San Francisco. Our tours were a mixture of Indian music and Sufi lectures and I was pleasantly surprised to discover the intensity of the young students in learning about the eastern music and philosophy. Two venerable swamis, Trigunatita and Paramananda, invited us to give a concert at their Hindu Temple. They presented us with a gold medal and kindly invited us once again to give a lecture on Sufism. After returning to New York I gave a few lectures at the Sanskrit College. That's where I met Baba Bharati, who, you are probably aware, brought the love of Krishna to the Americans. To my great delight I also met Mr. Bjerregaard—a student of Sufism, who was also the head of Astor Library. He was of great help, lending me free access to Sufi literature in his library. He told me he is writing a book on Sufism and Omar Khayyam. I should be talking about music and poetry in life, but I digress. Ah, my Sharda, since I would be returning to New York soon, may I speak with Pierre, begging him for your hand in marriage?"

"When you are leaving?" Ora Ray seemed to awaken from a trance, her question some lone cry from the wilderness in her heart.

"Soon, my Sharda, everything is happening so fast." Hazrat Inayat Khan began, "A few concerts at the Carnegie Hall in New York, then we are scheduled for a tour in Europe. That's why I am thinking we should get married, so that we can travel together." He paused, noticing her sudden distress. "If you are afraid of my speaking with your brother face to face, my Sharda, I would send him a letter from New York. Is that appropriate?"

"Yes, that would be fine."

"I would write to you every day," Hazrat Inayat Khan murmured tenderly, though his heart for some nameless reason was thundering.

"And yet, my Daya," Ora Ray used this endearment for the first time, "you are going to Europe. You have found not enough friends or encouragement here in America, is that it?"

"Your friendship alone is a world to me, my Sharda." Hazrat Inayat Khan smiled wistfully. "To satisfy your curiosity on account of Americans, I find them most sociable, friendly and agreeable. They are affectionate and very generous. Quick to respond to the idea of universal brotherhood. Avidly open to study any religion or philosophy. Their broad outlook has given me great hope and faith that their spirit of freedom, in time, would bring the idea of oneness to the view of the whole world. One great idea of disarmament started by the President Harding and embraced by all Americans is most commendable. This shows the bent of American mind. Besides, to their friends or enemies in trouble, whenever the occasion has arisen, America has most generously come first to their rescue. They also have great love for knowledge, search for truth and tendency to unity. America, so full of life, goodwill and enthusiasm, though still in its childhood, will became a youth who will lead the world toward progress."

"Keeping in view this future of a bright America, I must be going." Ora Ray stood up reluctantly. "It's awfully late and I am afraid Pierre would get suspicious. I have been going home quite late since the past couple of days and the maid told me he is keeping tab of my coming and going."

"I would be your nightly escort as usual." Hazrat Inayat Khan to got to his feet.

"When you are leaving for New York?" Ora Ray turned toward the door as if sleepwalking.

"Don't be afraid, my Sharda." Hazrat Inayat Khan couldn't suppress his own sadness. "We would get married soon. I would write to Pierre."

1912 ~ Agony Supreme

Before you judge my actions
Lord, I pray you will forgive
Before my heart has broken
Will you help my soul to live
~Hazrat Inayat Khan

Hazrat Inayat Khan had disappeared like a beautiful dream, leaving Ora Ray alone and forlorn. She had become a prisoner in the home of her brother since she had confessed her love, and Pierre had made sure that she would not ever be able to contact Hazrat Inayat Khan. Pierre, though outwardly open-minded and strong proponent all things Eastern, was infuriated by the very thought of his sister falling in love with an Indian mystic. He felt betrayed by Ora Ray as if she had committed some heinous crime by keeping her love secret, especially when she could be the queen of the elite society, not married to some alien Sufi and Musician.

Heartbroken and suffering the agonies of separation, Ora Ray in return felt betrayed by Hazrat Inayat Khan who seemed to have vanished in ether, not even responding once to her barrage of letters she had sent for the past couple of months. Yet, she could not believe that he would abandon her. She could always feel his loving presence inside the very core of her soul whenever her heart was bruised with grief and loneliness. Even when her torment was overwhelming and she could see herself drowning in tears of pain, she still could feel his all-embracing love comforting her, the voice within a distant murmur. *Don't weep, my Sharda, we would be together.* She would then feel consoled, wipe her tears, and write another letter, not knowing that she would ever hear from her love lost and precious.

And yet Ora Ray had risen above her grief and loneliness. She could not doubt his sincerity, always keeping the gold-nugget of her own faith in his love and promise close to her heart. Hazrat Inayat Khan had told her once that in fond remembrance of his Sufi Teacher he could never forget his simple words of blessings which proved to be most precious of his possessions, bringing him manifold joys in all his endeavors. His Sufi teacher by the name of Madani could not tire of blessing him with these words: *May you be blessed in faith. May your faith be strengthened*. Hazrat Inayat Khan in return had bestowed the same blessing upon Ora Ray and she clung to this blessing of faith amidst her rare moments of doubts and of countless heartaches. This faith alone in her Daya was her lamp of hope and strength. What kept her going was her own love boundless for the man who had elevated her to the status of a goddess. She had begun to think that few precious moments spent with him were a lovely dream, and now this heartrending separation another painful dream, which would manifest into mystical dream-state of happy reunion.

Pierre had forbidden Ora Ray to communicate with Hazrat Inayat Khan, but his harsh edict could not impose restrictions on the freedom of her thoughts and imagination. She was not living, but existing between the states of delusion and lucid clouds of reflection. Amidst the islands of clouds in her psyche, she could hear a clear warning. The ears of her heart were open, informing her that her letters were not reaching her beloved. Desperate to find means to communicate, she was succumbing to despair and depression. To escape such dark states of misery and to while away hours of loneliness, she had begun copying down her own letters written to her Daya, keeping one to herself with the hope that she would show them all to him when they were finally able to get together.

Several weeks later, some sort of hopeless, helpless pain had gripped Ora Ray's heart. She meditated for an hour, then tidied up her room as was her wont. Her next routine was to tidy Pierre's room, which she always found in much disarray since he spent most of his time in Yoga Academy. She stood in her room thinking of going to her brother's room, but a sudden longing in her heart was dictating its own command to write another letter to Hazrat Inayat Khan. A dull sense of poetic inspiration was gnawing within her as she opened one drawer searching for a blank sheet of paper. Instead, she found a bundle of her own copied letters to her Daya stashed in a listless heap. She scooped a few and sank into a nearby chair to read one which might bring her close to her love lost.

My Daya,

Could not find a chance, my love, to write you these few days. And how long it has seemed to *Sharda*, only God knows. Oh, my soul, my soul, how can I ever live through this separation and how is my Daya? If I could only know that, but it seems that I am writing to the winds, for it will still be a month and a half before I can hear from my loved one.

I shall try to tell you, My Own, how this separation came about. You remember the Saturday I was with you and all evening until one o'clock and Sunday all day and all evening, in fact the last days I saw my Daya. The next day I saw my brother, and someone had told him I was away, so he wanted to know where I was and what was the reason I came home so late? Of course, I told him what falsehood I could. Well, he could not understand how I could possibly be out so late and really thought I must be doing something wrong. So, he said he would have my trunk moved over to New Jersey and I need not go to New York. Adding, unless I wanted to, or if I loved someone in that city. Then he would do all he could to help me, if that person whom I love is in love with me also.

I knew then that he knew and that I could not communicate with my Daya again unless I told my brother, yes, I was in love. And remembering that he has always lived up to this word with me in everything, and remembering that my Daya has always said, *If we could only have my brother's consent, it would be much better.* I thought the only thing to do was to tell him that I love you and want to marry you. And yet, I couldn't bring myself to confess. He talked incessantly, almost for nine hours I believe, from morning until evening. Finally, he convinced me that he had great sympathy for me, and after all if I loved someone, I should tell him and he would not mind, *it matters not who he is.*

After I told him, he was livid with anger, saying, *Your blood will never mix with his.* Oh, my Daya, I cannot tell you what all happened, but he said he would not let you live. When these words were spoken, I felt myself going backward in a faint, but I held to consciousness as best I could. Thinking he might go over and kill you. So that night, Monday night, I would not go to bed and tried my best to run away, if only to warn you of your danger.

Well, my brother sent for several people that night and the whole house was in an uproar. Will tell you more next time, my Love. I must stop now. And when you are well, I will tell you why my brother would rather have me die than marry you. But, my Love, I must say I am thankful to God that I did tell him. For if we were married and gone away, I am positively sure that he would have found us and killed you. For he told me so and I honestly believe it. He said I saved your life by a hair's breadth. He destroyed all my clothes which I had worn during my music lessons with you, and many more things. I will tell you later, my Daya.

Meanwhile, love and thousand kisses from the saddest girl in the world.

Tears were running down Ora Ray's cheeks as another letter slipped down from her trembling fingers. She retrieved it; her heart somehow glowing with a warmth of strange consolation.

My Love,

My first letter to you was written on the fourteenth of August—that being after two and a half months after our last happy meeting, during which time I was ill. Yes, Dearest Heart, these poor feet should have some consideration as you wrote once long time ago, I don't even know when and why, for they have stumbled many times to mail letters to you when they were not strong enough to hold this body upright. You see, my energy was so low that it took several months before I gained some semblance of strength. The least exertion would exhaust me, therefore, the first month or so I wrote to you, my Love, under many difficulties, as it was so hard for me to be alone. I was watched so closely, you know. But I do not wish to worry you with such things—

A few of the letters Ora Ray had grabbed rustled down over the carpet, her soft white hands trembling as she sat there sobbing inconsolably. An astonishing sense of peace enveloped her after she had drained her sorrow in tears. *What did Daya teach me? What was his message? If I can recall that, it might heal the open wound in my heart. Lord, give me hope, understanding.* Ora Ray's thoughts were prayerful, her tear-streaked cheeks glistening against the shafts of sunlight streaming through the window as she sat there contemplating. The ears of her heart were open. She could hear the voice of her soul, or was it the voice of Hazrat Inayat Khan's soul? His tender, soothing inflections closing the wound in her heart with utmost tenderness.

The Sufi sees the truth in every religion.

Ora Ray was feeling the pulse of memories as if Murshid was speaking to her alone in the great halls where he gave lectures.

There are no barriers of race, creed or religion. Sufism is not a religion, but rather a way of life that enhances and fulfills every religion. This is not a new religion, or a new message. It is the same message of unity which have been given to humanity again and again, yet few hearts are open to grasp this message.

The Sufi Movement is a group of people belonging to different religions. Their love is in life as the love for God and humanity, instead of for a particular sect.

The principle work that the Sufi Movement has to accomplish is to bring about a better understanding between East and West and between the nations and the races of the world.

The need of the world today is not learning, but how to become considerate towards one another. To try and find out in what way happiness can be brought about, and in this way to realize that peace which is the longing of every soul and to impart it to others. Thereby attaining our life's goal, the sublimity of life.

Ora Ray's thoughts were shuffling back and forth from lecture halls to discourses in private homes. On the topic of God Realization Hazrat Inayat Khan had said:

There is one God, the Eternal, the only Being. None else exists save God.

There is one Maker, the Guiding Spirit of all souls, Who constantly leads all followers towards the light.

There is one Holy Book, the sacred manuscript of nature, which truly enlightens all readers.

There is one Religion, the unswerving progress in the right direction towards the ideal, which fulfils the life's purpose of every soul.

There is one Law, the Law of Reciprocity which can be observed by a selfless conscience together with the sense of awakened justice.

There is one human Brotherhood, the Brotherhood and Sisterhood which unites the children of earth indiscriminately in the Fatherhood of God.

There is one Moral Principle, the love which springs forth from self-denial, and blooms in deeds of beneficence.

There is one Object of Praise, the beauty which uplifts the heart of its worshipper through all aspects from the seen to the unseen.

There is one Truth, the true knowledge of our being within and without which is the essence of all wisdom.

There is one Path, the annihilation of the false ego in the real, which raises the mortal to immortality. And in which resides all perfection.

Ora Ray's thoughts were turned to another page, that of Sufi Path, described by Hazrat Inayat Khan to a hall full of avid audience.

Sufi Path is built by the knowledge of unity. This path serves as a religion of love and wisdom, so that the bias of faiths and beliefs may of itself fall away. The human heart may overflow with love, and all hatred caused by distinctions and differences may be rooted out.

To discover the light and power latent in man. The secret of all religions, the power of mysticism, and the essence of philosophy, without interfering with belief or customs.

To help to bring the world's two opposite poles, East and West, closer together by the interchange of ideals and thoughts that the Universal Brotherhood may form of itself. And men may see unity with man beyond the narrow racial and national boundaries.

The wound in Ora Ray's heart was bleeding no more. In fact, it was sealed with the knowledge of healing. Her eyes were opened, so was the window in her soul, reflecting a bright lamp at the altar of her heart longing for the glimpse of her Beloved. A subtle, astonishing sense of peace she had not experienced since the past few months was cradling her body in the warmth of luxuriant bliss. The very air in her room was filled with the loving presence of Hazrat Inayat Khan. She was lifted to her feet involuntarily. Some tender whisper in the wind was urging her to play music, to live, to hope, to rejoice. *Sharda,* one musical note of a caress was teasing the strings of her heart on the silken route to recovery.

Feeling giddy, Ora Ray was drifting toward the room of her brother, as if tidying up his room this morning would be a joy. She couldn't tell if she was under some spell or falling prey to the lure of some wild imagination. Pierre, as usual, had left his room in utter neglect, cluttered with magazines and newspapers. Slowly and neatly she made several piles beside his bed for his later perusal. A sense of urgency she had not ever felt before was following her, along with it the former sense of peace which she had felt but a few moments ago was leaving her as quickly as it had arrived. The old wound in her sealed heart was ripped open. The agony of her spirit so violent in longing for her Daya that she almost tripped over the pile of mail her brother had left on the carpet.

Scooping all the sealed envelopes in both hands Ora Ray reached for his bedside table where he usually kept his mail. Her heart was still throbbing, the agony of not ever finding Hazrat Inayat Khan plunging her once again in throes of despair and hopelessness. So overwhelming were the pincers of grief clutching her heart that she thought she was dying. For some strange reason she was focusing her attention on the bedside table laden with a coffee mug, an almost empty glass of water, and some old clippings from newspapers. She pulled open one drawer, but before she could drop the pile of letters in, her gaze fell on a scrap of paper with the name of her Beloved scrawled in his own handwriting. The letters fell from her hand to the floor as she retrieved that scrap of paper. She was dying again, she thought, but this time whipped by the breeze of fortune, for on this scrap of paper was Hazrat Inayat Khan's hometown address in Baroda, India.

Ora Ray had begun to believe in miracles, her heart was swaying in relief and her faith in love was strengthened. She was endowed with the beauty of this knowledge that, yes, she would be reunited with her Beloved. It was a sign given to her by the divine Providence. She would write to her Daya on this new address. He would answer. The voice of certainty in her was singing. They were fated to be united as he had told her repeatedly.

Sharda

It was the song of her Beloved inside the very altar of her heart she had not heard for so long, and now it was a palpitating symphony.

1913 ~ Glorious Wedlock

Before my eyes are covered
Will you let me see your face
Before my feet are tired
May I reach your dwelling place
~Hazrat Inayat Khan

Waters of mercy were Ora Ray's companions on the ship she had boarded from Philadelphia to meet her Daya in Europe. Her perfect faith in Hazrat Inayat Khan's love for her had lent her the gifts of intuition and perception to proceed in the right direction. She had written to him at his Baroda address in India. The relatives of Hazrat Inayat Khan had received this letter and they had forwarded it to his London address where he was residing while in between his lectures and concerts from Paris to London. Profoundly and gratefully relieved at finally hearing from his Beloved, Hazrat Inayat Khan had posted his own letter to one of his mureeds, Mrs. Eldering in New York to be hand-delivered to Ora Ray.

***

Months of grief, misery and hopelessness were wiped away by the magic wand of love as soon as Ora Ray received the much longed-for letter from her beloved Daya. Tears of joy and relief had flown freely from her eyes as she had read the letter over and over again to make sure that her Daya was well and alive. As promised, Hazrat Inayat Khan had sent Pierre a letter requesting Ora Ray's hand in marriage, but his request was most furiously rejected. Heartbroken, he had sent several letters to Ora Ray, but most probably Pierre intercepted all those and not even one reached his beloved Sharda. Pressed by the urgency of his tight schedule in Europe of giving music concerts and propagation of Sufi message, Hazrat Inayat Khan, along with his cousin and brothers, had left America in a state of utter despair. He hoped that soon he would return to

America to find his Sharda and vowed that he would not leave until they got married.

Meanwhile, Ora Ray had been too ill to write after that violent outburst of her brother when she told him that she wanted to marry Hazrat Inayat Khan. By the time she regained strength and started sending him letters, Hazrat Inayat Khan was already in Europe, traveling from Paris to London and overwhelmed by engagements in giving lectures and concerts. He, too, didn't receive even one single letter of hers posted at the New York address, though always longing to be in touch and to somehow snatch her away from the hold of her brother.

Ora Ray, after receiving that precious letter, was quick to secure a personal Post Office Box number in Tenafly, New Jersey, away from the reach of her brother's overwhelming surveillance. Now she was able to write to her Daya.

Dear Heart,
Could you not have put a different name on your envelope's return address, so that your real name would not be seen outside, then my brother would have never known I was receiving letters from you.

Now that the channel of communication was open, a stream of letters were exchanged between Ora Ray and Hazrat Inayat Khan until she decided to elope to get married to him in Europe. All her travel plans were made by her alone in utmost secrecy lest she be detained by her brother or worse, forced to stay in America. She consented to be a part of the social gatherings whenever Pierre wished, and it was during one of those Country Club theatre evenings that she slipped out unnoticed. As arranged beforehand, she took the train to Philadelphia and after boarding the ship never left the safety of her private cabin. She was grateful of the privacy, for all her meals were brought to her by her sole request. So blissfully happy she was to be free at last to be united with her Daya that time for her became a quicksilver dream on the wings of Pegasus.

During this journey Ora Ray wrote poetry within the confines of her cabin, read Hazrat Inayat Khan's letters countless times over, also copies of her own letters she had written to him, just to test her state of exaltation that she was not dreaming. Her precious possessions on this journey were a bundle of letters and one silver toilet set, exquisitely carved. She could not tire of reading her own letters either, but switching from one to the other, catching only snippets.

It would be two months before I leave for Europe. I think it best that I take a steamer at Philadelphia on my return to New York. So, my Love, with these late plans of going west it will not do to write my folks that I have committed suicide, for they may receive the letter before I could board the steamer. I think it best just to disappear. Taking my trip with a few things as it is natural in traveling and leaving my trunk at the station. They will locate my trunk and may perhaps think that I have been killed by some man, or that I may have been abducted in some way or other, and for some purpose as you oft times read of some crimes.

Of course, I know they would go to so much trouble and it may appear in the papers in order to locate me. But, my Love, if you really want your Sharda, you can have her. I will come to you no matter what happens. If you can trust your landlady, it is well for her to meet me, but in that case, I would be going to Paris, direct. My Love, do you not think it best for me to stay in London for a while. Paris would be the first place they would look for me. My love, and it is sure that my brother knows where you are, you being in public life and my brother could easily locate you.

Dear Heart

My brother even knew your last address at the last place where you were in New York. He even knew of the short illness you had there before you recovered. How he knew, I do not know? Someone certainly told him.

She also sent him a poem in one of her letters:

Far away is my Daya
My heart, my soul, my life, my all
Sad the day that parting came
Where is my love, where is he now
Just to see his face again
His voice to hear, his lips to kiss
I would die a thousand deaths
Where is Daya, where is he now

Another time a brief note by Ora Ray:

Love has a will and a will has a way, so there is much hope for us. May the iron bonds of love keep our hearts always together and I am sure our bodies shall unite sooner or later. Who could be so heartless as to keep us apart very long? My eyes are blind with tears, my Love. Goodbye, goodbye.

Ora Ray's last letter to Hazrat Inayat Khan before she left America:

My Love,
You will receive this letter about two weeks before my leaving, so I do not think it necessary for me to cable. After reading this letter you will know that I will be departing here about February 28 and I would rather cable you under another name if I receive word from you in answer to the letter I wrote you about it. If not, then I shall cable you InayatKhan, Varma, Paris. But wherever I land, my Love, you would have someone other than yourself to meet me, for I am afraid of making a scene at the landing. You know I have not regained my health yet, and my excitement may cause me to faint, as I did in the past summer, owning to my weakness. I do not know what might happen, so I would rather have our first meeting indoors. My Love, we must not have any trouble there. Dear Heart, did Mohammad Ali receive the Xmas candy I sent him? I think this—my fifty-fourth letter be the last one you answer, dear Heart, so there will not be any letters coming here after I leave.
Goodbye, dear Heart, remember I shall be sailing in about three weeks.
Love and longing from your own.

Final message from Ora Ray:

Dear Heart,
I do not want to endanger your life. You must always be well guarded from the day I leave here and when I arrive on the other side. You must not see me. For I am sure my brother will have detectives trying to find me

.

Hazrat Inayat Khan wrote to her that she must land at Antwerp, Belgium. He cautioned her that London ports were riskier with more chances of being detected by her brother's detectives.

The journey of dreams was coming to an end as Ora Ray opened the pothole of her cabin. The ship was being anchored at the port of Antwerp. Her heart was leaping out of her breast to embrace the cool night air, the crisp ether and the very heavens.

Hazrat Inayat Khan, leaving all caution to the winds, had come alone to receive his Beloved. Tall and handsome, dressed in his gold-brown woolen robe, matching his gold-lit eyes and neatly trimmed beard, he looked every inch a great mystic of the east. His dark, wavy hair draped over his shoulders were giving him the aura of a prince from the Arabian Nights. A full moon was suspended high, burnishing the waters to silvery brilliance. A procession of happy stars appeared to lower a confetti of lights as Ora Ray descended down the dock. Her white features looked waxen under the moonlit night and the brilliant blue in her eyes lit up to the fire of the sapphires at the sight of her Daya. The gold in her hair turned vibrant against a sudden gust of wind.

Ora Ray had landed on the beautifully lit port of Antwerp in Belgium and before she knew it she was swept into the loving arms of Hazrat Inayat Khan. He held her close to him as if he would never let her go, their hearts thundering in unison.

"My Sharda, my very own Sharda." Hazrat Inayat Khan murmured this endearment, his lips grazing her forehead reverently.

Two days later Ora Ray was married to Hazrat Inayat Khan at the Civil Register Office at St. Giles in London. She was registered as Amina Begum, her new title of high rank. Hazrat Inayat Khan's cousin and brothers arranged a small reception to celebrate this royal wedding. Not as elaborate as they would have done in India, but quite elegant in comparison with the limited funds they could spare out of their labor of love for music in giving concerts.

The wedding bliss which Ora Ray as Amina Begum experienced was beyond expression. She thought she was transported from the dungeon of the material world to heavenly abode where the angels sang glorious songs and where no grief or separation from Beloved existed. Each moment was filled with so much love. She was avidly conscious of the delightful activity all around. This brilliant flame of energy was from the very core of Sufi lectures, of music concerts, of lighthearted gaiety of Murshid's cousin and brothers, joking and laughing. Murshid was her beloved Daya, the happiest of all, now that he had found his Sharda, the sun-gold in his eyes getting brilliant each passing day during his lectures and music concerts.

Days slipping into weeks and months were inspiring and entertaining for Amina Begum. She was meeting great poets, thinkers and writers in London, amongst them one Indian poet by the name of Rabindranath Tagore. Also, an Indian poetess by the name of Sarojini Naidu.

Murshid kept Amina Begum by his side wherever he went, regardless of hectic schedules from Sufi lectures to music concerts. One of the noteworthy events during those evenings was a reception given by Mrs. Beatrice Irwin at the Literary Circle of Monico by Port's Club. The hall was teeming with the poets and the musicians: Cecil Scot, Percy Grainger, Mr. Streeker of Angener & Company. Amina Begum was particularly impressed by a gentleman by the name of Dr. King of Brighton who showed great interest in the Sufi Movement of the Murshid. While they were talking, another gentleman by the name of Lord Dunsany joined in, wanting to learn about the Symbology of the Sufi Poetry. Dr. Troller, who had previously taken Murshid on a visit to the London Conservatory of Music, also joined their circle, delighted by Amina Begum's charming conversation. The evening was full of surprises, for Amina Begum was being introduced by her husband to the elite of the literary circles in London, especially impressed by one friendly couple Basil Mitchel and his wife as if she had known them for a long time.

Mr. Strangways was one of the members amongst many belonging to that elite circle. He was also an author and a musician, writing a book on the Indian music. Miss Maude MaCarthy was a young English lady who was such an accomplished singer that she could sing even songs from South India. Mrs. Kumar Swami, another English lady, was the first European artist in London who had given performance playing Indian instruments.

Murshid and Amina Begum were ready to leave when Mr. Strangways stalled them, requesting a few moments of their time and attention. Earlier, Murshid had given him materials and information for the book he was going to write about the Indian Music.

"Mr. Khan, thanks for the information I needed for my book." Mr. Strangways smiled genially. "On another note, I regret to say that our people do not go much for art and music. In art, French are the foremost.

My sincere advice to you is to return to France. French people will find much interest in your music, especially in Paris."

"Many thanks." Murshid smiled back, shaking his hand gratefully before turning to Amina Begum and offering her his arm most gallantly.

"My Sharda, you would love France as I did," Murshid murmured, as they left the great hall. "It would be our home, our haven."

"My home is where you are, my Daya," Amina Begum whispered back, leaning on his arm blissfully.

"Before we leave London, I must take you to the Indian Club in Cromwell where I gave a lecture on music." Murshid appeared to be inhaling the scent of her sweet presence.

***

Within a month short of one week the newlyweds were in Paris, Murshid already booked ahead for lectures and concerts along with his cousin and brothers. They had rented an apartment and soon were astonished to find a policeman at their door. He was inquiring for a young American girl who had 'run away' from his family. After he was assured that she was legally married in London, he left apologizing for the inconvenience.

"Were you afraid, my Sharda?" Murshid asked after the police officer had left.

"No. Your Vadan-spiritual teaching has killed my fear. In fact, I wrote a poem about Vadan. Would you like to hear it?"

"I was hoping you would read one of your poems to me one of these days," Murshid intoned eagerly. "Of course, Vadan means eloquent speaker which I am not if you must know. But I am waiting for your poem. Won't you recite it please? Great pleasure, entirely mine, to hear it."

"A small one, I have memorized it. I can even read it in my sleep. Here it is." Amina Begum began with great enthusiasm.

O Vadan, thou art my favorite
A message sent from above
I carry thee as an amulet

Brought by the heavenly dove
I lay thee gently on the altar
My worship, to Thee, bequeath
Yea, I take Thee to my sepulcher
Forever, Thy word, I breathe."

"Oh, my lovely Sharda, you are a great Sufi poetess." Murshid clapped his hands with a childlike happiness. "Greater than the Mistress of the Sufi Masters as Rabia of eighth century was called, Sufi Mistress, born in the city of Basra in Iraq."

"Greater than that I would be a mother of your child just eight months away," Ora Ray exclaimed.

"My Sharda, my soul, my sweetness." Murshid caught her in one tight embrace, hugging and kissing.

1913 ~ City of Lights ~ Paris

Before I wake from slumber
You will watch me, Lord, I hold
Before I throw my mantle
Will you take me in your fold
~Hazrat Inayat Khan

Paris had become Amina Begum's home and haven, buzzing with the lights of enthusiasm to welcome the Royal Musicians. Though, the newlyweds were not alone in their home, sharing it with Murshid's cousin Mohammad Ali and his brothers Mahboob Khan and Musharaf Khan. Yet the cousin and the brothers were very considerate, collectively making it possible that the newlyweds had their privacy despite the constant stream of performances and Murshid's lectures shifting from venue to venue with very little respite in between. Amina Begum had learned early and rather quickly to share her husband not only with his immediate family, but with his mureeds, followers and admirers. If the popularity of the Royal Musicians was reaching its giddy heights, Murshid's lectures were attracting patrons and students to enhance the cause of the Sufi Movement. Parisians flocked to Murshid, avid, as if hungry for even a few morsels of knowledge and the concert halls were always teeming with the lovers of music wherever the Royal Musicians performed.

Amina Begum accompanied her husband to lectures and music concerts and often found herself amidst the presence of the great personalities. Murshid was much sought after by the literary and musical circles of Paris. Amongst the great personalities, she was particularly fascinated by the two opera singers, Emma Nevada and her daughter Mignon Nevada. Another lady who impressed her was Mata Hari who became her mentor in teaching her about the Indian culture. Amina Begum also learned how to wear a sari from Mata Hari. She loved the feel of silk on her body, always admiring the gold border on each one which she thought matched her hair.

Murshid and Amina Begum had very little time alone for themselves, but aside from lectures and concerts, they could not possibly decline the dinner invitations in the private homes of the famous musicians and composers. A couple of great composers, Debussy and Alexander Niklaye had become their best of friends and they frequently dined with them, discussing music and Sufism, also introduced to one Indian student there by the name of Mehtab who could play Dilruba—an Indian stringed instrument from the east region of the Indian subcontinent. Amina Begum was finding charming little surprises about her husband every day, one most delightful was that he could sing like an angel and used to make the Rajas and the Nawabs swoon with sheer delight in their royal courts with his voice alone without even touching any musical instrument. When he resumed this practice of singing in Paris on selective occasions, the purity of his voice moved the audience to tears.

Amina Begum seemed to be living in the wonderland of magic and mystery. She once told Murshid that she was living on the center stage of her own beautiful dream, amidst so much abundance of love from her Daya that at times she felt drowned in its essence of joy and fragrance. His response was that if he was to be allowed to stay in her dream, he would be blessed million times over in worshiping his beautiful Sharda until eternity. Each moment had become eternity for Amina Begum, and in her rare moments of solitude, she enjoyed playing veena and writing poetry. She loved attending Murshid's, lectures on music which were arranged by a Sufi student by the name of Kismet Stam who affiliated with the Oriental Dramatic Production. Kismet Stam was the cousin of a Sufi Scribe named Khalifa Sakina Funee whom Murshid had honored with the title Nekbakht. Through Nekbakht, Amina Begum had the pleasure of meeting a great musician by the name of Mr. Walter Rummel. Kismet Stam introduced Amina Begum to more great Artists, amongst them the famous, Isidora Duncan, also a young mureed of the Murshid, Zebunnisa.

The very air in Paris was charged with the scent of euphoria and since Murshid was gaining mureeds and admirers from all quarters, he decided to invite some of them at home for dinners and discussions. Usually weekends and late evenings were reserved for such pleasant repast and Amina Begum was the most gracious of hostess', presiding over good food and great conversation. Those were the times when she could feel floating in air with her Daya on a carpet of spirituality, watching the whole world transform itself into one big loving family. She enjoyed the company of all the mureeds, but a couple of them became her favorite, Monsieur Aillet and a poet Monsieur Jules Bois. Murshid, too, became close with those two, going as far as discussing his book, The Message of Spiritual Liberty, which was still an unedited manuscript. Strangely enough it was already being translated by Mlle Jorys from English to French. Amina Begum had taken charge of editing the manuscript when Murshid was practicing music or immersed deep in meditation. She was not only editing but imbibing great knowledge in realms both the spiritual and profound. The entire manuscript began to live in her head, and she began to contemplate this life while sweetly and gratefully aware of the new life in her womb. Her contemplations lent her the freedom to choose, while her will allowed her to select randomly.

Truth:

So many castes and so many creeds. So many faiths and so many beliefs. All have risen from ignorance of man. Wise is he who only truth conceives. Different methods called religions and philosophies have been adopted by different nations at various periods. Though the form and the teaching of several religions appear so unlike, their source is one and the same. But from the very beginning the differences have created envy, prejudice and antagonism between men. Such dissensions occupy a large portion of the histories of the world and have become the most important subject in life.

A wise man realizes that the fundamental basis of all religions and beliefs is one. The truth has always been covered by two garments: a turban on the head and a robe over the body. The turban is made of mystery known as mysticism, and the robe is made of morality, which is called religion. Truth has been covered thus by most of the saints and the prophets, in order to hide it from ignorant eyes, as yet too undeveloped to bear it in its naked form. Those who see the truth uncovered abandon logic and reason, good and bad, high and low, new and old. Differences and distinctions of names and forms fade away, and the whole universe is realized as nothing other than truth. Truth in its realization is one; in its representation it is many, since its revelations are made under varying conditions of time and space.

A water in the fountain flows in one stream, but falls in many drops, divided by time and space, so are the revelations by one stream of truth. Not everyone can comprehend the idea of different truths being derived from one truth. Common sense has been so narrowly trained in this world of variety that it naturally fails to realize the breadth and subtlety of a spiritual ferret beyond the reach of its limited reasoning.

Each month merging into another of healthy pregnancy was a source of great joy for Amina Begum, but not as great as compared with Murshid's who seemed to be walking on heavenly waters in paradise, singing songs of gratitude to his beloved God when away from his beloved Sharda. Since Amina Begum had grown heavy with child, he wanted her to rest more and not expend her energies by attending his lectures and concerts. He himself had cut down on his activities as much as he could and started giving his Sharda private lessons at home in Sufism.

"If anyone asks you what is Sufism? What religion it is? You may answer: Sufism is the religion of the heart, the religion in which the most important thing is to seek God in the hearts of mankind.

The Sufi message is the message of the day. It does not bring theories or doctrines to add to those already existing, which puzzle the human mind. What the world needs today is the message of love, beauty and harmony. The absence of which is the only tragedy of life. The Sufi message does not give a new law. It wakens in humanity the spirit of brotherhood, with tolerance on the part of each for the religion of the other, and with forgiveness from each for the fault of the other. It teaches thoughtfulness and consideration, so as to create and maintain harmony in life. It teaches service and usefulness which alone can make life in the world fruitful and in which lies the satisfaction of every soul."

As Amina Begum's stomach grew big with the quickening of life, Murshid's joy swelled over currents of love, fear and devotion. So concerned he was about the health of his Sharda that he became more gentle than ever before even when holding her in his arms as if she was made of glass and would break. His schedule was getting hectic again despite his efforts to cut down on his lectures and concerts so that he could spend more time with his Sharda and be close to her. But Paris couldn't have enough of him and Amina Begum insisted that he accept the invitations.

While Murshid was busy giving lectures and performances, Amina Begum stayed at home. She was beginning to feel the weight of her child and could not sit for long and didn't want to heighten her Daya's concern, knowing that he would worry too much even if he witnessed a trace of her pain or discomfort. She was enjoying writing poetry again in the hours of her solitude, besides, Murshid always left a copy of his lectures with her before he left in case she wanted to read. And read she did along with his book Minqar he had given her which he had written six years ago during his stay in Hyderabad in India. This book was about the composition of Indian music, including illustrations of various dances. While trying to understand she could not help telling Murshid that she was bewildered by all those terms of Tals and ragas as explained in the book, yet most impressed by his poetic expression which she needed to digest and explore. Sufi path of love was the road she could walk without stumbling, yet wanted to know what he meant when he said:

The noble Sufis are the swimmers in the ocean of Truth. The sound Kun — 'who' still echoes in their ears. They thrash their arms and legs in deep water, plunge into annihilation and safely wash up on the shore of immortality.

Marvelous is the state of an intoxicated Sufi
By the sound of pre-eternity
His milieu is neither land nor sea
The devotee of sweet song has been, since the day of pre-eternity
Fallen at the foot of the Beloved
By practicing godliness, it manifests in the soul
Whether I find myself in an idol's temple
Or the Kaaba's precincts
Inayat has sacrificed his whole being in sound
Prostrate since post-eternity at the Beloved's door
All that he requires is mere coarse meal

The Phenomenal and the Real are inseparably linked
Inayat, enough of you and this matter
The talk of reality and the circumstances of yours
The Sun is just a minute particle of God's kindness
Where there is kindness, hope blossoms forth

Amina Begum had read this poem of her Daya over and over again, but had difficulty understanding until he explained further.

In simple terms, my Sharda, the sound of music is in each particle of the universe. In the wind, in rain, in thunder and lightning. Even within the silence of the cosmos if one could hear such sound of one's own soul with the ears of the heart.

Immersed deep in her beautiful world of love, Amina Begum didn't notice the flight of time. Neither did she notice that her husband's renown was breaking loose from the seams of the Paris literary circles and expanding abroad globally, to the very gates of Russia.

A Russian Socialist, Princess Bartinoy, after attending a concert of Murshid in Paris had invited him to come to Moscow to meet the great Russian poets, artists and musicians. Murshid had forgotten about this until he got a formal invitation from the Maxim to perform in an Oriental Night Club in Moscow. Before accepting this invitation, he broke this news to Amina Begum with a flourish of challenge, seeking her approval.

"My Sharda, our precious gift of love, if you approve, would be unwrapped over the hearth of Russia."

Amina Begum had no objection. All she wanted was to be with her Daya wherever he went. Before leaving Paris to Russia she scribbled her own poem in her diary.

The mysticism of sound
Is a study most profound
In its depths Truth is found
O ye Seekers
Tarry not in idle play
But prepare ye for the day

Whence departeth soul from clay
O ye Seekers
Soar thou upward to that light
All pervading ever bright
Purified, in love, unite
O ye Seekers

1913-1914 ~ To Russia With Love

My heart is capable of every form
A cloister for monks, a temple for idols
A pasture for gazelles, the votary's Kaaba
The tablets of the Torah, the Quran
Love is the creed I hold
~Ibn al Arabi

Against the blue green oriental domes the Kremlin walls, with their ice-capped shadows, had captivated Amina Begum's heart under a spell of poetic bliss. As it did Murshid's heart, too, always a lover of beauty in nature and architecture. They were welcomed into a five-bedroom house called The House of Obidin on the corner of Petrovka Street and Krapivenski, just opposite the Vusoko Petrovsky monastery, only a kilometer and a half from the Kremlin. To Murshid, this house was a welcoming surprise indeed since it could accommodate his cousin and two brothers and still afford him the privacy with his wife, already in her seventh month of pregnancy.

Moscow, with its rich heritage in cultural diversity, was tailor-made for embracing and enjoying the exotic music of the Royal Musicians. The palpitating warmth and enthusiasm of the Russian audience would often draw Amina Begum into joining the late-night repast and parlance even when she felt tired and knew that her body demanded rest and quietude. At first the musical performances were at the nightclub of Maxim, but soon the Royal Musicians were inundated by so many requests to perform at the large concert halls that they would feel hard-pressed, not being able to accept all the invitations.

Amidst tides upon tides of musical performances within a few short weeks, Murshid was introduced to the literary elite in Moscow, amongst them Sergei Tolstoy, the son of Leo Tolstoy. Together, they devised a plan to combine eastern and western music for the performance of a play Murshid had written. He had borrowed the plot from the episode of Kalidasa's Shakuntala and named it Shiva. Sergei's friend Vladimir Pohl harmonized the Indian melodies for this play and even scored those melodies, creating ambience for a small orchestra. The theme of the play was the liberation of the soul. Amina Begum couldn't resist watching the entire play, sitting rapt, even forgetting the discomfort of her aching back caused by her swollen stomach.

Finally, she was constrained to stay home, her delivery time drawing close, but she was happy, anticipating the arrival of her precious child. Though tempted to go, she stayed home, even when Sergei took Murshid to Petersburg to meet the Tsar Nicholas II. Though she didn't get to meet the Tsar, she was delighted to learn from her Daya that Sergei Tolstoy had decided to become representative of the musical section of Murshid's Sufi Order in Moscow.

Before Amina Begum could be completely confined to bed, she took the opportunity of accompanying Murshid to the Ethnographical Museum where he gave a lecture to a large audience on music. After the lecture, she met a poet by the name of Mr. Ivanov whose wife was so impressed by Murshid's lecture that she promised to translate it word by word into Russian at the earliest opportunity. Amina Begum was utterly exhausted when they reached home and Murshid was very concerned, advising her not to tax her body with unnecessary exertion until the baby was delivered. He promised her that he would share every little detail of his activities every evening when he returned home after his lectures or concerts.

The Royal Musicians were in great demand and heavily booked for performances, so Murshid had employed a Tartar woman as a nurse for Amina Begum to keep her company while they were away. The nurse was to stay in service after the baby was born for the comfort of the child and the mother. Though good natured, this big Tartar woman somehow frightened Amina Begum with her idiosyncrasies, yet she grew fond of the nurse as the time of her delivery approached closer.

As promised Murshid had entertained Amina Begum every evening with each little detail of the acquaintances he had made or with snippets of parlance he could remember which he thought would delight her, including his active progress in gaining more mureeds. Within a span of few days he had accomplished more than he did in a few months in Paris. The highlights of one of his accomplishments was when he was invited to the Imperial Conservatory of Music where he had the opportunity of expounding the ideal of Indian music with musical illustrations. His new acquaintances were Princess Sirtolov Lavrovsky who had introduced him to the Principal of the Conservatory. He was invited to visit the Imperial School of Opera and Ballet, also meeting a music teacher of friendly disposition, Madame Switalovsky.

***

A dusting of white snow had mantled Moscow in a fuzzy blanket on the Eve of New Year. Murshid had returned late after his performance, but then as was his wont sat entertaining his Sharda with each little detail of his experiences away from home. He had been invited to a friend's house where he met the great singer by the name of Chalipin. Sergei Tolstoy also came, bringing along with him an army officer by the name of Henry Balakin. Murshid was impressed with the gentle manners of this officer and befriended him heartily. Henry Balakin was also keen in translating Murshid's book, A Sufi Message of Spiritual Liberty, into Russian. With this bulletin of news ended the New Year's Eve for Murshid and Amina Begum, as she was lulled to sleep cradled in his arms.

New Year Day, the Kremlin walls now draped in curtains of snow as if heavens itself was lowering confetti, was welcoming the baby girl born to Amina Begum. Murshid's joy was on the rungs of ecstasy, it was obvious, so profound and boundless that he rocked his daughter in his arms, singing and capering in the large bedroom while Amina Begum lay on her bed exhausted. She watched her husband's joy with great delight, her own heart glowing with love so bright that she could feel its brilliance inside the very altar of her soul.

Murshid named his daughter Noor-un-Nissa, meaning light among women. Amina Begum called her Russi, meaning born in Russia. This precious bundle of love was their little Princess, Noor, Russi, Babsy and Babuli—meaning father's daughter. Amina Begum was regaining her health and strength while enjoying the soft comfort of her Babuli with awe and gratitude. She still was not ready to accompany her husband to lectures and concerts, though he was busy once again more than ever before, always true to his promise of relating his experiences during the day to his Sharda in the evening. He had adopted a new ritual of singing to Noor morning and night as if she could absorb his love in her little heart, beating so tenderly against his own, brimming with song.

Noor was a happy, healthy baby, infused with so much love by her parents that she slept soundly the entire night through as if blessed with rare, caring spirit not to disturb her parents. When Murshid sang to Noor, the brilliant stars in her eyes seemed to twinkle with laughter and when he began talking with Amina Begum, she would be lulled to sleep. Murshid was in the habit of describing his friends to Amina Begum with such vividness that she thought she had met them somewhere previously. One of them was a Finish philosopher, Dr. K. W. Lybeek. He used to drive Murshid in a sleigh to a mysterious monastery close to their house. After coming back, Murshid would tell Amina Begum that in that monastery he met quite a few monks or priests of the Greek Orthodox Church. He said there was only one woman in that monastery who knew English and served as a translator. Murshid talked about Sufism to

Monks or priests, he couldn't tell the difference in their demeanor or appearance. They were impressed by his Sufi talk, but expressed wonder how truth could, outside their Church, exist in such perfect form as Murshid presented.

The truth was that Murshid lived this truth and enjoyed life, he had become expert in carving out time for his family, especially now when he couldn't wait to come home. To hold Noor in his arms and sing songs, to which she had begun to respond, smiling adorably. Noor was already forty days old and Amina Begum loved to watch the big father and little daughter locked together in silent conversation from heart to heart. Each day was a celebration for Murshid and Amina Begum and Murshid planned a special celebration, rather a ceremony, for Noor by inviting a few of his friends to dinner.

An elaborate feast was set up for the guests, but before that Murshid gently led Amina Begum to a couch against the velvet Portiere. She was wearing a blue sari and holding baby Noor in her lap, a bundle of frills and velvets. Beside her stood Murshid, tall and handsome. One of the guests told Amina Begum later that she thought she saw Nesterov's Blue Madonna against the dark red velvet portiere. The name of that guest was Yevgenia Yuievna Spasskaya and she enjoyed the entire ceremony with great interest. While Amina Begum sat holding Noor in her lap, Murshid's cousin, brothers and musicians came one by one, bowed low, sang a greeting and gave gifts to baby Noor. A tabla player by the name of Ramaswami was also a participant in this ceremony. He had met Murshid in New York and had kept in touch with him in Europe and was now in Russia. For this ceremony he joined the whole group of musicians and sang a beautiful song composed especially for Noor and Amina Begum.

Amina Begum, now blooming with joy and health, ventured out with Murshid as before, leaving Noor in the care of the Tartar Nurse. One evening after Murshid's lecture she met Professor Corsh, the great linguist of Moscow. She was also introduced to the ambassador of Bokhara who invited them to the house of one Amir in Bokhara. After dinner in the home of Amir they were introduced to Bey Beg the leader of the Muslims in Moscow, attended by many Tartars and a few men from Kazan.

The pulse of the East was in rhythm with Amina Begum's joyful heart when she accompanied Murshid to one of the concert halls where he was scheduled to give a talk about the subject of brotherhood, in combination with his musical performance. The hall was teeming with musicians, all delighting the audience with national tunes on their musical instruments. All were infused with great passion to display their talents, the Tartars, the Persians, the Serbians and the Bokharians, all united together in the musical language of oneness.

Amina Begum, in return, was imbued with the scent of poetic spirit within her and attracting the attention of great poets, too, one prominent one by the name of Skriabin. One singer by the name of Olga Turki was highly impressed by Murshid's lecture on Brotherhood and became his mureed. Aside from these joyful times, Murshid was becoming aware of the clouds of unrest hovering over the very heart of Moscow. The Tsar was perceived as weak and under the influence of his wife and courtiers. It was rumored that the anarchists and the communists were planting the seeds of discontent. The secret police of the Tsar were vigilant and suspicious. Even Murshid, his cousin and his brothers were under suspicion and followed by the secret police. Balakin, Murshid's trusted friend confessed to Murshid, to the chagrin of his own embarrassment that he was set by the government to spy on Murshid and his family. When Murshid assured him that it didn't matter and that he understood why he did it, Balakin requested to be accepted as his mureed and Murshid consented.

Added to this unrest was Amina Begum's shock and disbelief in discovering strange behavior of the Tartar Nurse. One evening she caught her feeding strong coffee to baby Noor. Another time she found her scrubbing Noor's body with a bristled brush. The most shocking of all was when she discovered that Noor's feet were tightly bound in doll-size socks. When questioned by Murshid, the Tartar Nurse who in fact adored Noor, broke into tears, sobbing inconsolably. Amidst her flood of tears, she was able to offer genuine explanations. Binding the feet of a baby was Chinese Tartar custom of keeping girl's feet small and dainty. Giving strong coffee was meant to strengthen the body and mind of the growing child. And scrubbing with rough brush was to massage the body so that it could withstand any climate if exposed to extreme temperatures. Instructed not to indulge in any of these practices, the nurse was all penitent and more loving than ever before.

The tides of great discontent were simmering inside the heart of Moscow, and the Tsar's officers came to Murshid's home, advising the Royal Musicians to leave Russia. Meanwhile, Murshid had received an invitation from the International Music Congress to perform in Paris in the month of June. Noor was barely five-month-old when Murshid and his family decided to leave Russia. The day they were leaving the riots broke out in Moscow and a horde of people erected a barricade, blocking their path at the very inception of their journey on the way to Paris.

Sergei Tolstoy had loaned Murshid and his family a sledge, but when the angry rebels blocked their passage, their carriage could not advance. Murshid was quick to act by drawing open the hood of the carriage while holding up baby Noor in his arms, standing tall and lofty. He was wearing a black hat, towering over his head high which looked imposing. His gold-brown cloak flapping around with a sudden gust of wind had stilled the crowd to an abrupt mode of awe, the sky itself suspended in silence against the canopy of bright stars on the dark blue horizon. The mob seemed to gasp for breath and parted, letting their carriage slip past the ocean of impending unrest.

Finally, Murshid and his family had carved their way from Petersburg to France. Amina Begum clutching Noor to her heart had heaved a sigh of relief. Murshid, holding both his wife and daughter close to him had murmured, "My Sharda, why do I see clouds of destruction everywhere?"

1914-1920 ~ From Paris to London

Love is nothing
Save grace and felicity
Love is nothing
Save heart opening and guidance
~Hakim Sana'I

    Amina Begum, with baby Noor as her greatest gift next to her Daya, was relieved to return to Paris. They had rented a house at Thirty-Nine Rue Singer in the very heart of Paris. Murshid was happy to arrive in Paris, too, especially in time to represent music of India at the International Music Congress. Paris was astir with the threat of looming war from Germany, but Parisian had yet not realized how it would affect their country or world at large in the grand scheme of warring nations. Before this threat materialized, Murshid received an urgent invitation from Switzerland to give a talk on Sufism in Geneva.

This was the first time Murshid was leaving without Amina Begum since the journey would affect Noor's health adversely as it already did during their travel from Russia to Paris. He didn't know that this was not the only time he would be leaving his family behind but would be constrained to leave them many more times in the wake of his distant assignments. Neither did he know that war would break out to disrupt the peace of the whole world. Meanwhile, Amina Begum, though Keeping Noor close to her heart as the most precious of her treasures, could not help missing her Daya, at times feeling subtle pangs of pain on the brink of anguished emptiness. To escape that feeling she would write to him passionate letters, this last one below a specimen of utter despair.

My Love,

I am wondering how you are today and when you intend coming back to Paris? My Precious, how I miss you, words cannot tell you. I know you must be suffering much, being alone and no one to help you and so much walking to do as you wrote in your previous letter. I hope you will never go alone again, my Love. Do write me a letter every day. I am always longing for your letters. I see nothing but clouds when you are away, my Own. My Precious, take good care of your pin, ring, etc., as it would be so bad to lose them. And in case you send your soiled clothes to the laundry, be sure to get them back before leaving Geneva. Do not leave them behind as they are your best clothes. Goodbye, dear Heart, take good care of yourself.
Always your most faithful,
Sharda

After receiving this letter, since he was already on his way to Paris, Murshid scribbled a short note in response.

Quite well, Murshid.

Murshid had written to Amina Begum earlier that he found Switzerland to be the most heavenly place on earth, telling her that finally he knew where God lived — in Switzerland. While in Geneva, he was inspired to start headquarters of Sufi Movement. He was overwhelmed by the warm reception accorded to him in Geneva, everyone so kind and welcoming. People came to him in droves to listen to his lectures, amongst them mostly wealthy and prominent citizens. Many of his lectures were held in the Swiss towns, followed by elaborate dinners in his honor exclusively.

It was a happy reunion to be back in Paris, keeping his Sharda close to him and not ever tiring of hugging and kissing Noor. His cousin and brothers were happy to have him back as their Master Musician, though he was spending more time singing to Noor than giving concerts. It was already August, wet and humid, and before the concert season could start with all its swing, news of war breaking out in Europe landed as a glacier of ice, German cannons aiming at Paris. The inception of WW1 was one whip of a warning.

London seemed to be a safer place than Paris, so Murshid and his whole family, already citizens of London, journeyed once again and took their residence at Ladbroke Road. The war was gaining momentum and the atmosphere of the whole nation was charged with the feeling of dread and vulnerability. Murshid was to face half empty halls during his musical performances, his income dwindling down to such deplorable low that he felt helpless and impoverished. The only abundance he could cherish and embrace was Sharda's love and Noor's precious smiles.

Travel was suspended during the onslaught of war, so despite their impecunious means, Murshid and Amina Begum spent happy hours together, Noor their greatest of delights. He would sing to his little Babuli and play music while she lay cradled in his lap, just like his grandfather who had raised him from cradle to youth with vibrant sounds of music from his veena. There were not many engagements for music concerts, but Murshid voluntarily sang for Gandhi once, who had tears in his eyes before Murshid had finished singing. He also visited the hospitals where the Indian soldiers lay wounded. To raise funds for the war widows, he helped arrange for free charity concerts.

New Year didn't bring any respite from the war, Londoners didn't have enough money to spend on entertainments. Yet, the Royal Musicians of India, after being in London for almost a year, were invited to play for the Opera Lakme, getting generous reviews in the newspapers. However, earning generous reviews didn't fetch them much money, so Musharaf Khan was constrained to look for menial jobs. Mahboob Khan had started giving private lessons in music. Mohammad

Ali was fortunate in finding work in the Music Halls, singing European Arias and ballads. Occasionally, the Royal Musicians were invited to play at the Art and Music Festivals, arranged by Richard & Wagner & CO by an International Theatrical & Musical Agency. Such assignments were not sufficient as means of good income, so Murshid and his family subsisted on dal and rice, at times only a loaf of bread.

During such times of hardship and impoverishment, one bright lamp of joy was suddenly lit to great effulgence when Amina Begum got pregnant with her second child. Murshid's heart was infused with such joy at this good news that his mind too was lit up with a sudden inspiration. He decided that he needed to establish a Sufi Order in London and came up with the idea of a symbol which would represent a winged heart inscribed with the star and a crescent moon.

Swiftly and astonishingly not only a Sufi Order and a Sufi Circle emerged, heralding the inception of a Sufi Center, the winged heart now a living entity. The Sufi Order, with its message of universal love, had begun attracting quite a few mureeds, amongst them one most devoted lady by the name of Raden Ayou Jodjana. She had taken music lessons from Murshid earlier and was eager to become his mureed. Murshid initiated her into the Sufi Order, also predicting bright future for her, which would later transport her to joys inexpressible, for she was destined to marry a prince from Java.

Raden's fortune, for the time being, was linked with the family of Murshid. Amina Begum was forever grateful to her for her selfless help and support with the household duties, from cooking to sowing to cleaning. Aside from doing household chores, Raden had succeeded in uniting a handful of mureeds as one single family. This family of mureeds united as one whole under the winged heart of Sufi Circle had accepted the responsibility of maintaining the Sufi Center, along with providing support to Murshid's family and assuring their livelihood. Regardless of her great contribution in securing comfortable living for Murshid's family, Raden continued to help in household duties, no matter how insignificant. So concerned she was about the privacy of the Murshid family that she took it upon herself to answer the door, not minding when other mureeds mistook her for a servant. Another devoted mureed was Madame Egeling, devoted to Noor.

For Amina Begum, Raden was her dearest of friends, sincere, trustworthy and loving. She kept Raden close to her when her time of delivery approached, trusting no one with the exception of her Daya. Amidst the sounds of bugles, drums and soldiers' marching steps on the hard pavement, Amina Begum gave birth to a baby boy. Holding dear the seal of ecstatic abandon, Murshid and Amina Begum named their child Vilayat, meaning born in the West. He was given the title of Pirzade, meaning son of the Pir. Noor, almost two-and-a-half-year-old, was a bundle of energy, excited to see tiny baby in the arms of her Abba, her father and in the arms of her Amma. She wanted to hug and kiss the wonder of wonders, this new baby whom her parents loved. She was told that Vilayat was her little brother, but she was to call him Bhaijaan, meaning big brother, him being the first brother.

The birth of Pirzade doubled the joys of Murshid and Amina Begum, Noor capering around with excitement to play with her little brother. Despite the raging of war with all its ravages of death and devastation worldwide, Murshid's sadness and strong feeling of helplessness was somehow transformed into spurts of inspiration after the birth of Vilayat. While Amina Begum was enjoying the bliss of newly found joy in her son, Murshid had decided to venture outside London to give lectures since recently the rules were relaxed and a little travel was permitted. To his great surprise he discovered that halls had begun to fill up for his lectures. The senseless war, so awfully prolonged, had created a need in the hearts of young generation to seek spiritual answers for all the grief and tragedies worldwide. More opportunities were opening for Murshid, and he succeeded in setting up a Chapter of the Sufi Order in Brighton, hoping to expand more when time and means allotted him such luxury.

Amina Begum called Noor the light of her eyes and now Vilayat became the light of her heart. Murshid's bright lamp was his Sharda and both the little ones the starry lights in his eyes which shone with great brilliance whenever he held them close to his heart, singing to them and feeling their heartbeats with joy.

Tragedies of war were felt everywhere and Murshid's family was not immune to sadness', but Murshid, his brothers and cousin worked hard to keep Amina Begum and the kids well fed and healthy, especially when Amina Begum had become pregnant again soon after the birth of Vilayat.

The government had rationed the food and they were grateful to get whatever was available, besides, even their combined incomes were too low to purchase anything in large quantities. The Sufi Order had gained popularity and Murshid was initiating more mureeds, amongst them one Miss Williams who also served as a secretary. Another lady by the name of Miss Goodenough also joined, who became devoted to the kids, also a great friend of Amina Begum.

Astonishingly enough, several months had scudded past and here in London, Murshid's family fell under the cover of false suspicion. The feeling of unrest as to Murshid's family being spied by the British government was lightened by the happy event of another starry birth. Vilayat was a little over two months and a year old when Amina Begum gave birth to a baby boy. He was named Hidayat, meaning a guide. Noor was told by her parents to call Hidayat Baiyajan, meaning little brother as opposed to Bhaijaan—big brother. Amina Begum, glowing with joy at the birth of her second son, was indeed a portrait of goddess enshrined within the mirror of Murshid's heart since he could not imagine anything more beautiful than his Sharda mantled in happiness. He, too, could forget about doubts, suspicions and ravages of war for a few moments now and then while he held his precious son in his arms. Noor could not be left behind, puttering around and demanding to hug and kiss her little brother, while Vilayat tugged at Murshid's robe for his attention. To commemorate this new birth, Murshid decided to set up another Sufi Center at the Harrogate. Miss Goodenough, who was given the name of Sharifa, had gone to Scotland to visit her family so couldn't be present for the opening of the new Sufi Center at Harrogate. As usual, he sang to his little ones and played music to forget the tragedies of war which seemed to entertain no hope of abating.

Noor, though little, was so loving to her brothers that Amina Begum thought she was an old soul who had always loved children. When she expressed her thoughts to Murshid, he laughed and exclaimed, "As far as I know she is a little theosophist!" With her dimpled, charming smiles, Noor seemed to be the only bright spark in keeping theosophy alive inside the hearts of all mureeds during the dark hours of war-torn England. During the second year of war, Murshid had stopped giving lectures at the Brighton Sufi Center, but the two of his mureeds remained devoted. One was Miss Hope and the other Miss Callow, both still visited him, more attracted by Noor than any prospect of seeing Murshid. Miss Goodenough had disappeared on some secret mission somewhere.

The Royal Asiatic Society started by Muir Mackenzie, too, owing to warring conditions, was unable to host any more of Murshid's lectures. However, quite a few of the Murshid's lectures were published by a Sufi Publishing Society established by Miss Williams. She had helped with the publication and the book was called, Pearls from the Ocean Unseen. Simultaneously, one of the Murshid's Diwan of Hindustani lyrics and the songs of India were translated by Mrs. Jessie Duncan Westbrook. For some reason, the warring years proved to favor Murshid's works being published and translated. Amongst those were *His Confessions,* written by Miss Miriam Bloch, and his own translation of the Rubaiyat of Omar Khayyam translated into English by Mr. Bjerregaard, who was his mureed from America and had followed him to London.

Amina Begum was the happiest when Murshid's book, *Pearls from the Ocean Unseen,* was published. She literally devoured the entire book, chiseling away time to read in between her household duties and her joys of motherhood. Not only did she read the book over and over again but couldn't stop re-reading until she wrote a poem about it to share it with Murshid.

O Pearls from the Ocean Unseen
Priceless and beyond compare
Long sought by many a marine
In earnest unceasing prayer
Thro' the depths of the waters pure
Various divers plunged to seek
Ye Pearls, until at last secure
In the hands of Him, so meek
He giveth ye to the world
To enlighten some few souls
With hearts waiting to be unfurled
By the message that consoles

There were conjectures that the war was coming to its end and soon peace would be restored. Meanwhile, Miss Goodenough returned to London and was given the new title of Khalifa, then promoted to Murshida. Amina Begum was grateful to Murshida Goodenough for her love to the family, especially for her dedication to Murshid for collecting and preserving his lectures with the intention of getting those published at the earliest opportunity. Another lady, Mrs. Benfon, was interested in Indian music and became a mureed. A couple of more wartime mureeds were Miss Khadija Young and Mrs. Hanifa Sheaf. Miss Williams, to soften the blows of war, began establishing a Theosophical Society in Southampton. Quite a few of the devoted mureeds ventured out to Leeds with the Sufi message where Miss Eileen fletcher took great interest in promoting the cause of the Sufi Movement.

***

The Great War which had begun July 28, 1914 finally ended No 11, 1918, flooding the streets of London with tears of joy. The sky, too, lowered pearls of mercy in likeness of rain pouring down in torrents. Amina Begum was happy to see the light of relief shining in the eyes of the Murshid. Immediately, he began looking for the lecture halls to spread his Sufi message, his whole being brimming with the hope of success. After the war people were more receptive to his Sufi message of love, peace and harmony. His music, too, was comforting, much like a soothing balm to allay the grief of many who were laden with the weight of pain for the loss of their loved ones, seeking solace in concert halls and learning afresh to embrace entertainment. New Year's Day arrived with a special fanfare since it was Noor's fourth birthday and Amina Begum could afford to celebrate it with cake and candles. Murshid's joy was boundless as he watched his precious Noor glowing with delight while unwrapping her presents.

Peace and prosperity had taken wings on the chariot of time. Another splendid New Year birthday had arrived for Noor. She had turned five and was royally treated with a party and lots of presents. She had been asking for a baby sister and Amina Begum had assured her that her wish was to come true soon this very year.

Time had become a quicksilver stream after the war, and it was already the middle of year when Amina Begum gave birth to her second daughter June 3, 1919. Murshid could not contain his joy to have another daughter. Since he couldn't squeeze the little one to his heart, his joy overflowed by hugging and kissing Noor and telling her that this new baby sister of hers was the most precious of her birthday gifts. Noor, of course was ecstatic, to her childish heart her wish came true as her Amma had promised and now she loved her sister as much as she did her brothers. The baby was named Khair-un-Nissa and Amina Begum called her Mamuli—mother's child since Noor was Babuli—father's child.

Amina Begum was so happy with her little ones that she didn't even notice that her family was under suspicion by the London Home Office. Murshid, it became obvious, was under suspicion of being an Indian spy since he had met in London the National Leaders of India, Mahatma Gandhi and Sarojini Naidu. With the end of Great War, a movement for independent India had become a great threat to the Britain. One day, when Murshid was meditating in his room, an English policeman showed up at the house, insisting that he wanted to see the Murshid. Musharaf Khan, who had let the policeman in was in a quandary, but went to Murshid, apologizing for disturbing him in his mediation. Murshid, upon learning about the policeman, told his brother to let him come into the room. The policeman, feeling the great energy of the meditation room and the calm personality of the Murshid, was quick to apologize and left hurriedly.

That was the day when Amina Begum realized how precarious was their life and livelihood in London. Murshid, who was spreading the Sufi message openly, felt confined under the constraint of surveillance. Especially so, when a friend of Lord Lamington commented discreetly. "Murshid, in order to really succeed in England, one must do work quietly."

At the same time one faithful mureed in Southampton by the name of Miss Dowland advised them to leave England, offering generous help to get them settled in France. By this time Murshid had enough mureeds who were dedicated to the Sufi cause and willing to add funds for relocation of the Murshid's family. Most generous amongst them, one from South Africa. Another mureed offered them a vacant summer house at Tremblay-Sur Mauldre about twenty miles west of Paris, just past Versailles.

Khair-un-Nissa was only a few months over one year old when Murshid and his family left London on a small boat. Amina Begum was relieved despite the fact that the kids were seasick, knowing that they would be fine once they reached France. To comfort and entertain his kids, Murshid played veena and sang songs. At times, Amina Begum would lean against his shoulders, watching the silvery waves rise and fall and praying for their safe return to France.

1920-1922 ~ Heart of Europe

To my Sharda
As pure as the water
Of a gentle stream
As near and as dear
As milk and cream
~Hazrat Inayat Khan

The French haven offered to Murshid and his family through one of the mureeds turned out to be an illusion. The summer house at Tremblay-Sur proved to be cold and damp and not conducive for healthy living. Amina Begum didn't mind, she was content to be anywhere with her Daya and little ones, but Murshid felt his Sharda needed more space, since his cousin and brothers also lived with them. He looked for opportunities to earn money aside from spreading his Sufi message so that he could secure a comfortable home for his beloved wife and children. Already Paris was responding quite favorably to his Sufi message and opening its halls for his concerts and lectures. Eager and welcoming crowds greeted him wherever he went, and his fame reached all over Europe. The door to opportunities was wide open, it soon became obvious, when he received an invitation from Baron von Graffenreid to give lectures in Geneva with the possibility of setting up a Sufi Order in Switzerland.

Murshid was reluctant to leave as that meant leaving his family behind, but Amina Begum encouraged him to accept the invitation. She knew that she and the kids would miss him, but her love didn't want him to miss this golden opportunity. Murshid left alone for Switzerland, not realizing that from now onward he would be constrained to travel alone than to stay with his beloved family in Paris.

***

The first lecture that Murshid gave in Geneva at the University for the Society was instant success, earning him more engagements. While giving a lecture at the public meeting in Salle Centrale, Murshid attracted the interest of Pasteur Charles Martin who initiated the establishment of the Sufi Headquarters right then and there at the premises. The first Sufi Headquarter was established at Salle Centrale and like-minded people from different faiths and countries came to exchange ideas and ideology with the Murshid. One lady by the name of Bloomfield was the representative of Bahaism. Mrs. Bartram and Dr. Netobi were from Japan, affiliated with the International Movements on behalf of the League of Nations. Monsieur de Traz, a Swiss writer was very much interested in the Sufi Message. Murshid gained many admirers and mureeds, especially after his address at the Hotel d' Angleterre arranged by Madame Lavanchy and Frau Schroeder in Lausanne. The new mureeds amongst his admirers were Nina Mitchell, Baronesses Van Hogendorp, Mr. Fouad Selim Bey Alhigazi, and Countess Pieri. When it was time for Murshid to leave Geneva, Murshida Goodenough came from Paris to Geneva to take charge of the Sufi Headquarters and serve as a General Secretary.

Amina Begum was happy to have her Daya back at home in Paris. In his absence, Amina Begum had grouped their children as Rubies Four and he was delighted to hear about this new title, entertaining his precious jewels with song and music. Also anxious to share his experiences from Switzerland, he was devoting a couple of hours alone with his Sharda every evening, trying not to miss any details which might be forgotten by him, but would be stored in her memory-book forever. Every evening was a session of snippets and they enjoyed their solitude together before he got too busy giving lectures and concerts.

The first snippet was plucked from the soil of London since Mr. Clifford Best, who had started work in establishing a Theosophical Society in Southampton, had sent his brother Shabaz Cecil Best to Switzerland to be accepted as mureed. Murshid had ordained him as Cherag meaning lamp, and had sent him to his family in Brazil, instructing him how to spread the Sufi message. Back in Switzerland his students had collected one-liner quotes from his lectures, compiling those in a book form and getting it published in England. Before he left Switzerland, they had presented to him that book as a token of their gratitude, it was titled Bowl of Saki. Amina Begum wanted to know everything about Bowl of Saki, so he was always delighted to expound to her its origin and significance.

The Arabic word Saki means wine-server or wine-pourer and is frequently used in Persian poetry to describe the glorious Server who continually pours out the wine everlasting to all of mankind, while implying that only a completely empty bowl is truly ready to be filled with such a fine wine. For the Sufi, the greatest task of life is to become empty enough, selfless enough, to be a suitable receptacle for the wine which the *Saki* pours.

What makes the soul of the poet dance? Music. What makes the painter paint beautiful pictures, the musician sings beautiful songs? It is the inspiration that beauty gives. Therefore, the Sufi has called this beauty *Saki* the divine Giver who gives the wine of life to all.

The Bowl of Saki in Sufi terminology is also linked to the power of the mystical glance. Besides its precious work, which makes the eye superior to every other organ of the body, it is the expression of the beauty of body, mind and soul. Sufis, therefore, symbolize the eye by a cup of wine. Through the eyes, the secret hidden in man's heart is reflected into the heart of another. However much a person may try to conceal his secret, the reader can read it in his eyes and can read there his pleasure, his displeasure, his joy, and his sorrow. A seer can see still farther. The seer can see the actual condition of man's soul through his eyes, his grade of evolution, his attitude in life, his outlook on life, and his condition, both hidden and manifest. Besides, to the passive soul of a disciple, knowledge, ecstasy, spiritual joy, and divine peace, all are given through the glance. One sees in everyday life that a person who is laughing in his mind with his lips closed can express his laughter through his glance, and the one who receives the glance at once catches the infectious mirth. Often the same happens through looking in the eyes of the sorrowful, in a moment one becomes filled with depression. And those whose secret is God, whose contemplation is the perfection of beauty, whose joy is endless in the realization of everlasting life, and from whose heart the spring of love is ever flowing, it is most appropriate that their glance should be called, symbolically, the Bowl of Saki, the Bowl of the Wine-Giver.

When Amina Begum was satisfied as to what Bowl of Saki means, he shared this poem of his which he had written in Switzerland.

Thy light which riseth in my heart,
In the hearts of my mureeds may shine.
The juice that hath made me so drunken
O *Saki*, give my mureeds that wine.
Surround my mureeds with Thy beauty
Create in their lives harmony divine.
Give them sympathy for one another
Raise them above life's mine and thine.

Thy light which riseth in my heart,
May in the hearts of my mureeds shine.
The juice that intoxicated me so,
O Saki, give my mureeds that wine.
Surround my mureeds with Thy beauty
Create in them Thy harmony divine
Give them sympathy for one another
May they forget world's mine and thine.

Paris was abuzz with the homecoming of Murshid, and he was busy once again giving lectures and concerts. Amina Begum found herself entertaining French admirers of Murshid, the potential mureeds-to-be who frequented their home and participated in the Sufi discussions, besides being a gracious hostess. She got to meet Madame Detraux; Mlle. De Sauvrezis and Mlle. Gelis Didot who became her great friends. Some foreigners also came for discussion, a few amongst them, Monsieur de Roibul, Mme Frank Owska, and Mme Chestowsky. She also accompanied Murshid to attend a series of lectures he was scheduled to give at Musee Guimet. Stealing some time from his hectic schedule, Murshid was able to find a house in Wissous, hoping to accommodate his big family and a flux of mureeds whom his Sharda was always willing to entertain with generous dinners.

That house in Wissous rented from a naval officer, too, proved insufficient, but before an appropriate house could be found, the Royal

Musicians were getting invitations from Holland and Belgium to give concerts. Murshid's message of Sufi love, too, much needed after the devastating war, was reaching all over Europe. He was being sought by the universities and theosophists to deliver lectures on Sufism. Time had picked up speed once again, just a few months stay with his beloved family in Paris and he was on the road again, this time with his cousin and brothers to Holland and Belgium.

Rubies Four and his beloved Sharda were left behind in Paris and Murshid was feeling the pain of separation more intensely than ever before since his kids were at that age when he enjoyed playing with them, teaching them songs and music. Sadness had settled inside him, some subtle pangs of loneliness even amongst crowds, even when the Royal Musicians were received with great enthusiasm in Holland. His Sufi message, too, was received with delight and gratitude. Glowing reviews were posted in Holland newspapers in praise of his lectures and concerts. During one of his lectures arranged by the Theosophical Society, he happened to meet a Dutch Theosophist lady by the name of Mevrouw Egeling. So impressed was he by her advanced state of spirituality that he couldn't help initiating her at their first meeting. She was given the title of Fazal Mai—meaning Grace of God.

Grace of God continued to bless him with fortunes during his travels. In Holland he also developed great friendship with a loving couple, Sirkar and Saida Tuyll and succeeded in establishing a Sufi Society with four branches in the cities of Hague, Arnhem, Amsterdam and Haarlem. From Holland he was scheduled to travel to Belgium, but before he left, he added more mureeds to his Sufi Circle, De Heer Farwerek and Heer en Mevrouw Van Meerwijk. Another mureed who joined later, Heer Wegelin, was delegated to China to represent the Sufi Message since he had connections there and was very enthusiastic.

While in Belgium, Murshid had begun to feel the pain of separation more intensely than ever before since this was the place where he was reunited with his Sharda after an excruciating interval of wait and anticipation. He was giving lectures in Antwerp and Brussels to the eager audience of the Theosophical Society, feeling respite from his pangs of loneliness. Soon a Sufi Order was established in Belgium with the help of Maelemer Heris of the Star Movement, its board members Madame

Graeffe Van Gorckum; Madame de Sturler; Dr. Bommer helped to promote the Sufi message.

Despite being busy, Murshid always carved time to write to his Sharda. Soon he was giving lectures at the Student Club, in the home of Counte and Comtesse de Laka, and at the Society of Les Amis de la langue Anglaise, surprised to find there one of his old mureeds whom he had given the name, Zebunisa. One evening at the Palais Mondial he met Monsieur Piollet who invited him to dinner to meet his family, but he was so homesick that he declined. Instead, he went straight to his hotel and wrote a letter to his beloved.

My Heart, my Sharda,

How lost I feel without you. Soon I will hold you in my arms. You know the mureed who sent us the wedding invitation, could you please send this wedding wish from us on their wedding day.

May my best wishes reach you
On your wedding day
May your life be happy
From my heart I pray

Also please send this poem to the mureed who sent us a card announcing the birth of his son.

Welcome the son
My little sunshine
Bring to the earth
Some light divine
Eric Inayat
Edward is he
May he live long
And successful be

Most of all, my Sharda, Happy Birthday, I will be missing you. Please accept this little poem from the bottom of my heart.

The reward of good deeds
My soul and my life

The forgiveness of my sins
My Sharda, my wife
Soon to be with you and with Rubies Four,
~Your Daya

In response to this letter Amina Begum sent this poem, knowing that he would be coming home soon.

The honor of my virtues
My heart and my soul
The tolerance of my faults
My Daya, my God
~Your Sharda

Murshid returned to Paris much earlier than expected, lighting up his home at Wissous with lamps of joy and activity. Though this house was inadequate for constant flow of mureeds, Amina Begum didn't mind, feeling the energy of love enveloping everyone now that her Daya had come home from Europe. Rubies Four were the happiest of them all since Murshid was compensating for the time lost with his family and giving them extra attention. He had partitioned his time with great precision. Being the first one to rise in the morning, he would sit in his little garden and meditate for a couple of hours. By the time he came inside, his children were eager for his hugs and kisses and little anecdotes. Living room was their playground and the kids would never tire of requesting their father to sing and play veena, which he enjoyed himself besides entertaining his Rubies Four. Since Noor was the oldest, almost close to eight springs, Murshid had started teaching her Indian ragas while giving her lessons on veena. His afternoons were spent with his mureeds, Amina Begum his constant companion. She also accompanied him to all the concerts and lectures in the evenings. The most devoted mureed, Raden, had grown very attached to the kids and preferred to stay with them in the evenings, telling them bedtime stories before they went to sleep. Another mureed Madame Egeling helped with duties of the household.

Murshida Fazal Mai from Holland followed Murshid a few months after his return to Paris and she became a great friend of Amina Begum.

Every afternoon she came to their house along with other mureeds and enjoyed the hospitality of the spiritual host and the gracious hostess. She was a wealthy lady, very sensitive and considerate. The first thing she noticed in Murshid's home was lack of space for his big family, aside from droves of mureeds gathering in the living room always overcrowded. She wanted to do something to help the family but didn't know how to approach the subject without being intrusive and patronizing. From other mureeds, Kismet, Nekbakht, and Madame Egeling, she learnt that since Murshid was not making enough money to support his family by giving lectures and concerts, all the mureeds had secured his consent to accept their contributions. All mureeds in and around France had created a pool of funds to keep Murshid's family comfortable with growing needs of their children and education. Murshida Fazal Mai was not in Paris when such a pledge was made by the French mureeds, but an opportunity to help presented itself one day when she happened to be with the family on an excursion.

***

It was a balmy spring day and Murshid's family was taking a leisurely walk in the Bois de Boulogne in Paris. Amina Begum had straggled ahead with the three little ones while Noor and Murshida Fazal Mai stayed with Murshid. Noor was holding her father's hand and swinging it playfully, and he was indulging her in this activity with great delight, keeping rhythm and laughing. Suddenly, little Vilayat left his mother's side and raced back to his father, wanting to cross the bridge over the River Seine and climb the hill yonder.

Merrily, the whole family, fulfilling little Vilayat's wish, crossed the bridge and stood looking at the little hill admiringly. Amina Begum suggested that they walk around the hill since Hidayat and Khair-un-Nissa were not old enough to venture climbing. During their walk, Murshid came upon a house surrounded by trees. He admired it in silence. His eyes were suddenly lit up with awe as he noticed the Eiffel Tower in the distance, and he could even see the cathedral of Notre Dame from where he stood. In the background he could catch the subtle music of the River Seine winding its way around Paris. Amina Begum joined him, equally rapt and fascinated.

"A beautiful home, my Sharda, for us, and for receiving the mureeds, if we can purchase it," Murshid murmured wistfully, slipping his arm around Amina Begum's waist.

"It's for sale too, Murshid! Do you see that sign?" Murshida Fazal Mai couldn't conceal her excitement under a spell of inspiration. "I have been looking for a house, too, and this one is perfect. All I need is one room in the corner and the rest is for you and your family and, of course, if you want to receive the mureeds. It would give me immense pleasure just to think that this house would be lovely for your kids and for Amina Begum.'

"How can I ever thank you enough, Murshida Fazal Mai! And this house for my rowdy brothers, too." Murshid could barely voice his gratitude, unable to take his eyes off the gleaming windows on the upper story.

Noor had abandoned her father's side and had joined her three younger siblings to play at the foot of the hill. She was very protective of Vilayat, telling him not to dare climb alone.

"Can this be really true if I am not dreaming? Thank you, Murshida Fazal Mai!" Amina Begum sang with joy, the brilliant blue in her eyes enveloping Fazal Mai in rills of gratitude.

"We would call it Fazal Manzil, meaning the House of Blessing. You are very gracious, Murshida Fazal Mai." Murshid seemed to break the enchantment of his Sharda, he himself moved by the spontaneity of joy and love from the very being of Murshida Fazal Mai.

"I am glad I could help in some little way, Murshid. The pleasure is entirely mine." Murshida Fazal Mai could not help spilling joy from her very eyes. "A thousand-fold pleasure all the days of my life, knowing that I could live so close to Murshid and his loving family."

"What place is this?" Amina Begum was feeling like a little princess, caught in the mists of enchantment on earth and haloed by God's divine miracle from the very heavens.

"Only a few miles away from the center of Paris, this place is called Suresnes. If we walk a little further, we would see the Longchamps racecourse," Murshida Fazal Mai said.

***

Murshida Fazal Mai purchased the house at the end of Year 1921 and in early Year 1922 Murshid's family moved in, naming it Fazal Manzil. It was truly a house of blessing for everyone. Murshida Fazal Mai chose one room on the top floor, Noor and Khair shared one room and another one was shared by Vilayat and Hidayat. Mahboob Khan and Musharaf Khan shared one room while their cousin had his own separate bedroom. Murshid and Amina Begum had a large private bedroom of their own on the main floor. There was a large garden in the back where the Rubies Four played most of the afternoons while Amina Begum, Murshid, and Murshida Fazal Mai sat under the shaded grove of plum and apricot trees, planning to build a Sufi Lecture Hall on the vast grounds of Fazal Manzil. Murshid had already decided that after the hall was built, Murshida Fazal Mai would be the one presiding over the Universal Worship for guests and the mureeds.

Amina Begum was the happiest of them all in Fazal Manzil, always grateful of the luxury of spending private, intimate moments with her husband. She accompanied him to his lectures and concerts since devoted mureeds were always there, eager to play with the children. Noor was allowed to attend all the evening functions with her parents since she was now eight-year-old. She had started going to school in the local College Moderne de Filles in Suresnes. Murshid was still giving her lessons in Veena and singing and she was getting proficient, both in playing Veena and singing.

The children, including Noor, were naughty and Amina Begum wanted to be strict and discipline them, but Murshid's loving heart always over-ruled her judgment, requesting her not to scold or punish their little darlings. Though he himself devised his own unique punishments, like making them run around the garden ten times, or observing silence for a couple of hours, or sitting with their eyes closed in one corner. Fazal Manzil had become Amina Begum's bliss supreme and Murshid's earthly paradise. It also served as a spiritual retreat for all the mureeds and a learning center for the children who enjoyed the ceremonial aspect of the Universal Worship. Murshida Fazal Mai conducted the rites of the Universal Worship inside the large living room of the Fazal Manzil against the glow of candles and the fragrance of incense lulling all to a sense of serenity and camaraderie. Noor loved to attend these services, mature beyond her years to grasp the concept of tolerance for all religions, while her younger siblings were fascinated by the beauty of the rituals and the prayers.

As much as Murshid wished to stay in this blissful world of loving, living dream, he would be snatched away now and then to fulfil his duty of propagating the Sufi message outside the haven of France. Whenever he was absent, his absence was felt like a cold draft in summer season. Children would grow quiet and reclusive. Amina Begum would pretend to be cheerful to conceal her sadness from her Rubies Four, even Murshida Fazal Mai would feel empty and distraught. Noor was the most sensitive amongst her siblings and she missed her father the most. Yet, much like her mother, she could don the mask of cheerfulness, especially to cheer her mother since she loved her Amma as much as her Abba. The first time Murshid left was a few months after they had moved to Fazal Manzil, for he had received an urgent note from Switzerland that his presence was needed in Geneva where the Sufi Movement was going through the tides of transformation.

A group of mureeds in Geneva were happy to see Murshid, noting with great wonder that beyond their expectations, the Murshid was swift in bringing order and smooth out all wrinkles within the fabric of Sufi Movement. Murshida Goodenough was transferred from Geneva to Suresnes to help Madar-ul-Maham who was in sore need of a trained secretary. Monsieur Talewar Dussaq was then appointed General Secretary of Sufi Movement in Geneva and his sister Comtesse Pieri was given the post of General Treasurer. Monsieur de Cruzat Zanetti was appointed supervisor of the Sufi Movement. Despite the scenic beauty of Switzerland, Murshid was feeling homesick. He knew he wouldn't be able to return to France to celebrate his Sharda's birthday, so he sent her a poem he had written under some profound spell of loneliness.

At all my busy hours in life
Everything I do
You are my only consolation

And I think of you
My work keeps me away from home
But I leave my heart
At home, to be ever with you
Our souls can never part
Happiness be with our little ones
Right guidance from above
I wish good luck in our house
And my deepest love
Prosperity and success
Long life and good health
May be yours always Sharda
My treasure, my wealth
With a world of love
My Heart, on your Birthday, from your own
In response Amina Begum sent her own poem to him in Geneva
Day by day and night by night
Everything I see
I feel thy presence in it
And I think of thee
In everything I may do
Thy love guideth me
When thy gentle voice I hear
I am in ecstasy
While the Holy Deity
Watches over all
Eagerly I wait to hear
Thy whispering call, my Daya
Your own Sharda

Meanwhile Noor, endowed with the poetic talent just like her mother, designed her own card and wrote a poem for her mother's Birthday on behalf of her sister and brothers.

Dear Amma,
I wish you a very happy Birthday today. I wish I did not have to go to school today because it is your Birthday. And if we could all go out today to celebrate

your Birthday. We should go to Bois-de-Boulogne. But I have a gymnastic lesson and a sowing lesson, even on your Birthday.

Love from the four children
Good health
Long life
Right guidance from above
Prosperity
Success, happiness, and love

Amma Jan I wish you the happiest happy Birthday you have ever had, and I hope you will have no work to do but get out in the beautiful parks and play with us. And I hope Allah will make it a beautiful day and I hope you will have hundreds of presents and hundreds of birthday cards. With all the love and kisses from your loving little daughter.

Noor

A couple of weeks after Amina Begum's birthday Murshid returned to France and Fazal Manzil was imbued with the energy of love and laughter. Amina Begum's joy was boundless. Noor was ecstatic now that she had become adept in playing Veena, she was trying to teach her brother Vilayat, now only a six-year-old, though eager to play Veena. Hidayat had turned five, but he was too restless and not as yet inclined to learn any music. Khair was only three and cossetted by all, including Miss Raden and Murshida Fazal Mai. She had also become a darling of one of closest of friends of Amina Begum, known to children as Aunty Madame Peineau.

The poem Noor had written for her mother's birthday, she recited to her father proudly. So much activity at Fazal Manzil since her father's return that Noor barely noticed the flight of time. Already one and a half month had fled past and it was her father's birthday. So, she quickly designed another birthday card and once again wrote the birthday wish on behalf of all her siblings.

Dear Abba,

We all wish you the happiest Birthday possible today and we offer you this little vase for which we have spent all our money gladly for your Birthday. And we hope you will keep it always in your room in remembrance of your naughty little children.

Noor, Khair, Vilayat and Hidayat

A week later after Murshid's birthday, Amina Begum was taken ill with some sort of viral flue thought to be infectious. Murshid was very worried and, taking the advice of the family doctor, took her to one of mureed's home in Paris so that the kids didn't get infected as they were considered to be the most vulnerable. Murshid stayed with his wife, taking care of her and keeping her as comfortable as possible till she could recover and return home to Suresnes. He came home for brief periods to see the kids and Noor had a chance to send letters to her mom, one of those below made Amina Begum cry, though Murshid was there to comfort her with soothing endearments.

Amma Jan,

Every night we all ask Allah to make you quite well and strong and to bring you home quickly and safely. I know you are in Paris, but I don't know where. Please will you write and tell me where you are living. I am sending you these drawings of little children to remind you of us. When Abba brings me to you, I will bring you something that Miss Strauss has brought us. The children are very good and have been making photographs. With all the love and a hundred kisses.

Noor

Murshid was more like a mother than a husband to Amina Begum during her illness, reluctant to leave her side, feeding her with his own hands and monitoring her intake of liquids and medicines. He even read to her from his book, Bowl of Saki, at her own request. And she requested it often, for she said his soothing voice and pearls of spirituality eased her feverish discomfort as no medicine ever could. It was obvious his tender loving care made her recovery swift and in less than a couple of weeks she was able to return home to the utmost delight of her children. Fazal Manzil was abuzz with joy at Amina Begum's homecoming and mureeds were bringing home cooked food and fruit baskets, wishing health and happiness. Murshid was glowing with joy and relief and before retiring to bed Amina Begum poured more joy into his loving heart by giving him the surprise gift of a poem she had been inspired to write after his indulgence in reading to her from his Bowl of Saki.

> O Bowl of Saki! Blest thou art
> A treasure from the divine
> Each day thou bringest to my heart
> A token of love's pure wine
> From thee I learn humility
> Selfless love and sacrifice
> And lo! Thou givest me the key
> To the gates of Paradise

To my Sharda
As sweet as the honeycomb
As sacred as the Church of Rome
As pretty as the flower
Of lover's dream
~Hazrat Inayat Khan

Rubies Four were Murshid's precious jewels to gladden his heart more and more after Amina Begum returned home, though still in the process of recovery. At times she complained of shortness of breath, so he was strict in forcing her to rest longer and starting her on a regiment of healthy diet with supplements of nuts and fruits. Dr. Pierre Jordan and his wife visited often, not as much as for medical advice, but for moral support. Her health was improving each passing day and she had begun to host dinners for the mureeds in the evenings. Murshid was able to spend six happy months with his family, playing with his kids, enjoying lively conversations with his mureeds, and having the great pleasure of keeping his Sharda by his side during his lectures and concerts, before he was constrained to travel to America. Murshida Rabia had sent him a message that his presence was urgently needed in the US to maintain and strengthen the Sufi Movement with his lectures.

Murshid was reluctant to leave since he had grown quite apprehensive after the recent illness of Amina Begum, but she urged him to go, promising to watch her diet and to take plenty of rest as he suggested. The children, of course, were saddened by the very thought of their father leaving again to lands alien and distant. Besides, they would be missing his love and indulgence, playing with them, teaching them music, and singing along when they went for excursions. They were spoiled and they knew it, gloating in their little hearts that they didn't go to bed as instructed, hiding behind the banisters on the upper story, and watching all activities of late-night dinners with the mureeds. Murshid knew about such little mischiefs of his adored ones, but he didn't have the heart to scold them and didn't even tell his Sharda lest she reprimand them and rob them of their innocent pleasure in night adventure and secrecy.

Before leaving, Murshid had consulted with his friend Dr. Pierre Jordan and had requested Murshida Fazal Mai to make sure that Amina Begum went for regular check up to maintain good health. Leave-taking was difficult for all, especially for Amina Begum who could not help feeling a little sting of presage every time that Murshid was ready to travel abroad. He could feel her sadness, promising to write to her often, concealing his own sadness in a profusion of endearments.

The journey to America was long and tiresome despite the fact that he meditated and wrote new lectures on Sufi thought and Sufi Symbology. He was scheduled to go directly to New York, but his ship was diverted to Ellis Island. As soon as he got settled in his hotel, he wrote a letter to Amina Begum and posted it immediately.

My Sharda,

I am unfortunately detained here, as the quota for the Indians is full for this month in New York, so I am taken to Ellis Island. Glad to have this experience though, to see to what extent materialism has affected big nations. It seems contrary to the attitude of the ancients of welcoming a foreigner as a brother and treating him most kindly in every way, that he may not feel he is in a strange land.

As nothing disappoints me, this reception affected me but little. They would not have me any longer than a few hours only. I was to stand before a tribunal. They asked me many questions in connection with myself and my work. And I, whose nation is all nations, whose birthplace is the world, whose religion is all religions, whose occupation is search after truth, whose work is the service of God and humanity, my answers they found interesting, yet they did not answer the requirements of their law. In the end, one of my mureeds, Marya Cushing, who is arranging my visit to New York, came to my rescue and answered all their questions to their utmost satisfaction. They seemed in the end much impressed and embarrassed and immediately exempted me from the law of geographical expulsion.

My Heart, my Sharda

Be not anxious my Sharda
On His service I must go
Though parting is hard to bear
But it's God who meant it so
I'll carry you in my heart
Wherever in the world I roam
His protection is over us
Rest in peace, soon I will come

In response to his letter Amina Begum sent one of her poems out of many she wrote in his absence.

The highest inspiration
Beloved so true
The only consolation
My Daya, are you
If ever there is a pleasure
Searched the world through
If ever there is a treasure
My Daya, tis you
And now that life be over
Naught care I to do

But fly from earthly cover
My Daya, to you

Why I wrote this poem, I don't know, dearest, just want to share with you. My health is great. Rubies Four send their love, we all await your return.
Your Sharda

Amina Begum, though busy with her children and with a fleet of mureeds practicing Universal Worship under the guidance of Murshida Fazal Mai, could not get accustomed to being separated from her Beloved. She was feeling this subtle vacuum inside now more than ever before, since she could not help noticing that all the children missed their father. Especially Noor who had turned nine, and was mature beyond her tender years, sort of dreamy and thoughtful. Though she loved to play with her sister and brothers, at times she preferred to be alone. When visited by such moods of seeking solitude, she would crawl into her own private world of silence, playing planetary games and writing poetry. Amina Begum encouraged Noor to express herself in music and poetry, gratified to know that when she did, her sadness in the absence of her father was lessened. Meanwhile, Murshid and Amina Begum kept the flow of letters smooth and constant, not ever separated in thoughts. Murshid wrote in detail and Amina Begum was always grateful for his love and thoughtfulness.

My Sharda,

I gave lectures in New York for different societies interested in philosophical subjects and am glad to see again the smiling face of my friend in music, Dr. Reebner. My old mureeds, I don't think you ever met them, Mrs. Logan, Mrs. Eldering, and Miss Genie Nawn came to see me in New York and we had a delightful conversation. I am in Boston now, giving lectures to the societies interested in metaphysics. It was a rare delight to see Dr. Kumar Swami at the Art Museum of Boston. The only Hindu, I think, who occupies a fitting position in the States. Boston seems to me a miniature of England, the people are refined, cultured and reserved.

I hear Murshida Rabia is not popular in San Francisco. Maybe it is a race prejudice or that there is a spirit of rivalry and jealousy. Perhaps I expect more than what should be anticipated, still I cannot help it. I cannot be pleased with small success. My visit has given new life to the Sufi Movement in America and now I am sure it will grow.

You need to get strong, my own Heart. I hope you follow the medical advice of our friend Dr. Pierre Jordan without fail and do your breathing exercises every day. Now I have learned many American words and phrases and when I come home with my added accomplishment, you will be surprised to see the change. I feel America is the place to work, not France. Don't tell Murshida Fazal Mai— Budhi as you call her, she wouldn't like my saying America is the place to work. You don't like it either. But I love America, perhaps because I love you.

Your very own,
Inayat

Murshida Fazal Mai was a pillar of strength for Amina Begum since her health was not too good, though she wouldn't admit even to herself. She was lonely in the absence of Murshid and even the constant stream of mureeds visiting Fazal Manzil or staying within the precincts of Suresnes couldn't dispel the feeling of her loneliness. Murshida Fazal Mai, with the help of Madame Egeling, was in complete command of the Fortnightly Summer School which Murshid had started before leaving for America. Aside from the Universal Worship in the Oriental Room, Murshida Fazal Mai also presided over the meditation sessions. She was also negotiating a deal for the acquisition of land with the intention of building houses for the mureeds close to Fazal Manzil. The land she wanted to purchase looked like a small valley, perfect for the meditation of the mureeds.

While Murshida Fazal Mai had taken charge of the Sufi Circle, Amina Begum could devote more time to Noor who was having a difficult time in adapting herself in French-speaking school and needed to master French fluently. Vilayat, now seven, was bold enough to admit that he wished he had a father like other children. But then noticing the pained expression of his mother he kneeled at her feet, apologizing quickly and praying in earnest for the safe return of his father whom he missed terribly. Amina Begum hugged him tightly, consoling him that his father missed him as much as he did him, and that he would return soon. Her stream of love for her children always reached out to them to help and comfort, but to allay her own loneliness and self-assurance she turned to Daya's letters, reading many times over every evening.

My own Sharda,

From Boston I went to Detroit, then made a short visit to Chicago. I am in California now, this time of the year it is efflorescent with abundance of nature's beauty in blooms and fragrance. Mr. & Mrs. Wolf very kindly gave me a ride in their automobile from Los Angeles to San Francisco, a rare delight traveling at leisure. Murshida Rabia was thrilled to see me, introducing me to a host of mureeds to welcome me in San Francisco. Philip Hacket; Mrs. Havens; Mrs. Long; Dr. Barnes; Mr. Martin; Mr. George Baum; Mrs. Rebecca C. Miller; Hiss d. Hepburn; Mr. Samuel Lewis, if I can recall all correctly. Here I gave lectures at the Paul Elder's Gallery on music, poetry and philosophy. For the first time I went to Santa Rosa and paid a visit to America's great horticulturist Luther Burbank. I was delighted to hear him say, *I treat the plants as human beings and I feel among them as amidst friends*. I told him, to me it is a bridge between science and mysticism. At the same time, it is a promise that science in its full rise will someday be completed by mysticism. He told me he was trying to take thorns out of Cactus and wanted to know what I was doing. I couldn't help saying, I was trying to take thorns out of the hearts of men.

My Soul, my Sharda,

I am so glad now that you have a cook and a nurse for the children. I hope you will take the needed rest and the treatment which I sent in that doctor's prescription. My own, I am anxious about your health and you cannot help me better than taking good care of yourself. I received your letter, my Soul, and was afraid you will use that nurse for pressing clothes or doing something other than helping you to relieve you of your work that keeps you on your feet. I am realizing now every day that if we had a hundred servants to help, still you would work just the same, for work is your disease. It is most unfortunate that you ignore my advice and neglect your health. It is my devotion for you which makes me uncomfortable and anxious for your state of health. Soon, I will hold you in my arms, Sharda, stay well!

Amina Begum had finally started heeding her husband's advice, trying her best to improve her health before he returned to France. All the meals to be prepared for the family and for mureeds were entirely left into the hands of the cook. The nurse, too, was instructed to watch Khair and Hidayat when she was tired and sought much-needed rest after her duties of receiving certain mureeds. Hidayat was now six and loved to run wild in the garden and had to be constantly watched. Khair was only four, happily active and demanding constant attention. She was the darling of all the mureeds and they were glad to play with her and watch her play in the garden. In fact, the mureeds were rather possessive of all the children of Murshid and always caring and indulgent.

Murshid had returned home to France and Fazal Manzil was bathed afresh in the light of joy and love, filling the hearts of family and friends with lighthearted gaiety and carefree abandon. Amina Begum was glowing with the warmth of love and whatever little energy was lacking in her road to recovery, was replenished by the very presence of her husband, lending her the gift of perfect health. Noor could not have enough of her father, wanting a big chunk of his time all to herself. Though, she did relinquish this claim to her younger siblings who invaded their father's lap while she felt content just to sit at her father's feet. Vilayat, too, felt content, sitting close to Noor, quiet and unobtrusive, luxuriating in the rich tones of his father's voice whenever he sat down to talk about his travels in America. Since Amina Begum had traveled with him through his letters, he chose the places about which he had not written to her before leaving America.

The children didn't understand much about America or cherags as mureeds or even about Sufism, but they loved listening to their father, as if cherishing the vey aura of his loving presence. Amina Begum understood everything and silently blessed the loving family in togetherness. Murshid seemed to reminisce and somehow Rubies Four were lulled to silence when he started talking.

"I visited Santa Barbara on my way to Los Angeles. Murshida Rabia was with me and she is the one who gave a talk about Sufism before a little group in the home of our beloved Khalifa, Mr. Connaughton. He and his wife were made cherags. Another couple Mr. & Mrs. Wolff were made cherags along with their friend Mr. Edfar Conrow. At the Ambassador Hotel, where I gave several lectures, I found the audience most attentive, amongst them the most enthusiastic were Noor Jehan and Mrs. Sarah Wolff. During that time, I made friends with Mr. Mirza Assad Ullah and his son Dr. Farid. Some of my mureeds arranged for me to give lectures in Chicago where I met Mrs. Durand. Next, I was to go to Detroit, but before leaving I appointed Misses Bennetts as friends of our Sufi Movement in Chicago. Upon reaching Detroit I found that the most interested in my Sufi message were Mr. & Mrs. Lowe and Mrs. Hurst. Before I left for New York, Mr. & Mrs. Hobart were made cherags.

"I gave a series of lectures on Sufism in New York and then flew to Philadelphia where Sitara Coon made arrangements for me to deliver lectures on Sufism and Spirituality. Mr. White was very interested in our message, so I made him Cherag. Once again I returned to New York. Our representative in New York, Mrs. Marya Cushing founded a Sufi Order for students interested in Sufism. The work of this Order was entrusted in the hands of our Sheikh and Siraj, Mr. Shaughnessy. Mr. Cowley was chosen to look after the Sufi Movement in New York."

Amina Begum was enjoying having her Daya back and had started writing poetry again. She could afford this luxury of time and inspiration since Rubies Four had claimed their father as their sole possession and Murshid was delighted to teach them song and music and tell stories. Murshida Fazal Mai had taken full charge of the mureeds, so Murshid could devote more time to his family. In the evenings he devoted his time to his Sharda and sometimes she shared her poetry with him which delighted him beyond measure.

O Love, human and divine
Thou, inspirer of my soul
The tales of love unite me
With the object of my goal
Thou didst descend from heaven
To illuminate the way
For earthly souls that stumbled
In the dark and went astray

Amina Begum and the children barely had their fill of Murshid that he had to go on another mission abroad. A letter from Geneva arrived, written by Mr. Zanetti, that the Sufi Group in Switzerland was requesting his presence at an important occasion which would be explained after he arrived. Reluctant to leave as usual, but curious to know what the important occasion could be, he decided to make a short trip. Before leaving he assured Amina Begum and the children that he would not tarry long and would bring back gifts and the beauty of Switzerland.

True to his promise, Murshid stayed in Geneva only a week and sent a letter that he was on his way back to France. The important occasion he explained was that by the efforts of his mureeds the Constitution of Switzerland was revised, and the Sufi International Movement was incorporated in this same Year 1923 for the first time, according to the Swiss Law. Meanwhile Amina Begum was missing him so much that right after he had left, she had consoled herself with a high dose of inspiration.

Beloved what care I of these things
These gardens and palaces for kings
Tis true it was a rare and pleasant dream
For thou to share with me a life supreme
Would that in a humble little hut
Thou wert with me singing thy gamut
And I to wash thy feet in acquiescence
'Stead of a palace in my loneliness

1923-1925 Christmas at Fazal Manzil

Inayat, whether every phrase falters or not
The divine melody will resound until the Day of Resurrection
What form can be more beautiful than ours
Still, with all our delicate beauty, we mingle with dust in the end
As many dances as the stars and peacocks have
All of these movements are just ringings of the Truth
~Hazrat Inayat Khan

Fazal Manzil was the happiest place on earth, not only did Murshid and his family feel it to be so, but all the mureeds, too, and whoever came to visit, no matter friends or strangers. Murshid was back from Geneva and Fazal Manzil was imbued with the fresh scent of joy and energy. He mainly stayed in Paris, giving lectures, but occasionally traveled to Europe to preside over the retreats while striving toward expanding the message of Sufi Teaching. Amina Begum was the happiest ever, assisting Murshid with the Summer School in Suresnes. Though engaged in several activities, Murshid was successful in chiseling out time to give Veena lessons to Noor and Vilayat. Even Hidayat was keen on learning and four-year-old Khair seemed to imbibe the sound of music with a childish sense of joy and playfulness. She was enrolled in the same school where Noor was studying, but for some strange reason didn't like going to school. Later, Amina Begum discovered that Khair was having difficulty in getting adjusted in school, mainly because her name Khair-un-Nissa was too difficult to be pronounced correctly, so she decided to change it to Claire.

Claire was happy to have this new name, gaining new friends and beginning to enjoy going to school. At home, Amina Begum had to watch Claire closely since she was wont to run after her brothers over the large field across the road from Fazal Manzil. That large stretch of field also hosted abundance of shrubs and vegetation and served as a favorite hideout for Vilayat and Hidayat. Another of their favorite sports was to climb the plum and apricot trees whenever Murshid took them to the Sufi Lecture Hall which was still being built close to the grounds of Fazal

Manzil. At times, when some of his mureeds commented that Hidayat and Vilayat were naughty, Murshid would exclaim, *at that age I was worse.* He would then take his sons across the street from Fazal Manzil where one of his mureeds, Ekbal Dawlat was building his house. Most of the time Murshid's brother Mahboob Khan accompanied him to see the house in progress, most importantly to see Ekbal Dawlat's daughter, Shadi, with whom he got engaged.

This summer, after his return from Geneva, Murshid was getting to know his Rubies Four with the rare delight of a loving father since his trips to Europe were brief and his stay in Fazal Manzil longer. He was discovering new pleasures, taking his whole family to Paris for shopping. Amina Begum loved these family trips the most, especially the random shopping sprees when she was inspired to help Murshid decide and acquire various items for home or for the Sufi Lecture Hall. One-time, Amina Begum preferred to buy yellow curtains for the Sufi Lecture Hall and Murshid was delighted by her choice, saying I love this color of sunshine. In return, she would be giddy with delight when he purchased something rare or quaint, like a camel skin lamp or a Moroccan rug.

The children loved such objects which looked exotic or eastern and were attracted toward the Indian culture which their father described only in stories. Noor being the eldest was more imaginative than the rest, also more passionate and innovative. She loved to dress her sister and brothers in Indian clothes which her mother stitched gladly to indulge her beloved daughter in her whims and inspirations. On her own, Noor had initiated that she and Vilayat would write plays and then all Rubies Four would rehearse and perform. After a few days of rehearsal, they would proudly perform in front of their parents and a host of mureeds. Mureeds were the most avid of their audience, admiring the bright costumes of Vilayat and Hidayat in colorful turbans and Claire in baggy pants with a sequined frock. Noor would meticulously don herself in gold broidered sari and even make Amina Begum wear one which she wore at times anyway, loving the feel of silk on her body, also gratified since most of these outfits were gifts from Murshid. The summer was such a golden time of joys, imbued with Noor's self-directed plays and trips to Paris that time literally grew wings, flying past summer and fall into the cold womb of foggy winters.

Christmas was fast approaching and Fazal Manzil was decked with blessings countless and with abundance of joys and prosperity. As a child, Noor remembered a couple of Christmas' in England during the war and a couple of more in Paris which were not very impressionable. But this year's Christmas she was looking forward to since her father had told her that he was planning a beautiful surprise for the whole family. Noor was ecstatic, learning many things about Baby Jesus, especially curious about his being born in a Manger. When Murshid hung stockings over the mantelpiece, she wondered if Santa Claus was going to fill those with gifts. Imaginative as always and gifted with poetic inspiration, she began writing letters to Santa Claus. Amina Begum's eyes flooded with tears of joy when she noticed that Noor was helping her younger brother and sister to also write letters to Santa Clause, and when Claire was having trouble writing, she wrote one on her behalf in a quatrain.

Santa Claus do come to me
In your mantle white and red
Down the chimney come and see
Little me just tucked in bed

My dear Santa Claus

I would like a toy motor that I can sit in for Christmas. Everyone in Fazal Manzil believes in you but my Bhaijaan Vilayat.
Love and kisses from Hidayat
Please do not come through the central heat chimney, if not you will fall in the fire.

My dear Santa Claus,

I would please like a bicycle an Italian one like Leonardos' and one for everyone in Fazal Manzil and for the family of Mahboob uncle and I would like a violin also please. And a little piano only for me and an airplane and des sabots de Salieres.
Love and kisses from Vilayat Khan
And will you please go to tin-house to our neighbors.

Dear Santa Claus,

I hope you are well. I would like a little bicycle and a new pram and a big doll and a motor car that I can sit in and Baiyajan Hidayat is naughty.

Claire

My dear Santa Claus,

I would like to see you at Christmas. I would like a toy motor that I can sit in and I won't break it and it must have pebbles just like the ones I had before and I thank you for the things you brought last year.

Love and kisses from Hidayat

A dear old man is Santa Claus
Of course we all love him
He comes and brings such pretty things
And charges nothing, nothing

Dear Santa Claus,

I need a little writing desk and I would appreciate it more than any toy.

Love and kisses from Mamuli—Claire

I am a funny girl

Dear old Santa Claus,

We can never thank you enough for all your interest for little children. How happy we are when Christmas comes. There is a little boy in Italy who does not believe in you, but I have made him believe in you, so would you please go to his house—Porte-Pinciano Roma, his name is Leonardo. And there are two children Emile and Olivier who live in the little house just near our house, will you please go there if they are there at Christmas. And there will be in Suresnes a big Christmas tree for the poor children. Will you please go there in the Mairie Town Hall.

With all the love from Babuli—Noor

Would you please come and see us on Christmas like in England?

The Christmas finally arrived with much anticipated joy at the stroke of midnight. The Rubies Four in the likeness of four rubies with the fire of curiosity tiptoed the massive Oak staircase to reach the stately Oriental Room where the big surprise awaited them as promised by their parents.

And a wonderful surprise it was. A live Christmas tree lit by a myriad of soft candles. The Rubies Four were suspended in abeyance at the very door, rapt and dazzled by the twinkling of lights as if a whole starry sky was hugging this room in its light of peace and serenity. Trimmed in gold and silver, tiny treasures glittered on each branch. Deer, bells, fairies and cherubs, all exquisitely hand painted. Against the shimmering lights of the tree, crystal ornaments and little figurines had captivated all the children in a deep trance that they didn't even notice the presence of their parents.

Noor was the first one to espy her parents, her sweet Amma donned in a light-blue silver-broidered sari, sitting regally in a red-velvet chair. Her face was aglow with joy, her eyes radiant-blue and sparkling. Beside her Amma's chair stood Noor's dear Abba in apricot colored robe, his eyes equally bright and his face suffused with the purity of love. He held out his arms and Noor sailed toward him as if hypnotized. The other children followed suit, awakening from their spell of awe and wonder, and were received into the loving arms of their father. Amina Begum was doling out gifts to each of her Rubies Four, her eyes shining with so much happiness that they looked brighter than the brilliant-blue stars under the canopy of moonlit sky.

The happiest of all Christmas' was dissolved into the soft snows of New Year. Soon Murshid was busy giving lectures and several music concerts were scheduled. Engaged thus, he was happy to be home with his family, but that didn't last long, for he was being sought by other groups in Europe. Much in demand, he was finding it difficult to decline, in the beginning accepting only engagements for small periods of time. Amina Begum and the children were getting used to his brief absences but could not dispel the clouds of sadness which pervaded Fazal Manzil when Murshid was away on lengthy assignments. For one of those assignments he went to Denmark and gave a lecture at the English Club in Copenhagen. Then he was invited to Germany by Professor Goreke to speak at the Urania Hall. From there he traveled to Holland and was happy to see the Sufi Society flourishing in Hague. He was happily surprised to see his brother Mahboob Khan who had decided to get married with Shadi in Holland and he was fortunate to attend the wedding. After the wedding celebrations he went to Belgium, feeling homesick, missing his Sharda and children. Though busy with lectures and meetings, he wrote long letters, even sending long poems to his beloved.

> A most loving mother
> And a wife so true
> Most dearly Beloved
> My Sharda are you
> It's only your pleasure
> Which I try to do
> If I have a treasure
> My Sharda it's you
> All my success in life
> Who is credit due
> Who is my inspirer
> My Sharda it's you
> Many friends I have known
> But faithful are few
> And my only best friend
> My Sharda are you
> And when life is blue
> Who is always near me
> My Sharda, it's you
> Health, wealth and happiness
> To my Sharda give
> God always protect her
> And may she long live

Amina Begum always felt comforted by his letters. But after reading this poem she felt sad, knowing that how lonely he must be feeling in Belgium since that was the city they were reunited after long months of painful separation.

From Belgium Murshid journeyed to Geneva. He was also scheduled to visit the Swiss Center and give talks about Sufism. He had sent several letters from Switzerland, but his last letter before leaving for Paris made Amina Begum concerned and apprehensive. She was always worried about his frenetic pace in giving lectures and traveling, but now some sort of fear was clutching her heart about his health. This brief note below was the cause of her mounting fear.

My own Heart,

It is most difficult to bear the responsibility as I do and to pay due attention to everybody at all sides and yet keep one's balance. I am getting quite tired of this world.
With all the love there is,
Inayat

To allay her feeling of fear, Amina Begum had started reading her old poems she wrote as a teenager. The one that comforted her the most was in remembrance of her father.

Again I would run and leap in glee
My father eagerly watching me
No sweeter joy could ever be
If only dreams were true
Again the golden lane we'd stroll
My fears and tears he would console
An answered prayer to thrill my soul
If only dreams were true
Again those melodies, I would sing
My father's voice accompanying
Gladness in our home I would bring
If only dreams were true
Again I would sit down at his feet
His ancient tales to fondly greet
An earthly paradise complete
If only dreams were true

Finally, Murshid was back in Paris and his tiredness vanished magically at the very sight of his Beloved and children. Fazal Manzil was coming alive again with songs and laughter. Everyone was falling into the carefree routine of the summer. Murshid had started teaching Summer School and since it was on the precincts of Fazal Manzil, he had the time to furnish the much-neglected rooms in his own home for the comfort of the family. He was glad that the house of Mahboob Khan's father-in-law Ekbal Dawlat was complete and that he had already started building another one adjacent to his own for his daughter and son-in-law. Amina Begum had met Ekbal Dawlat before as an acquaintance, but now that he was a part of the family, she was getting to know him better. Now he became a frequent visitor at Fazal Manzil and Amina Begum found him to be jovial and affable, and he loved to play with the children.

Rubies Four loved to stay with Ekbal Dawlat when their parents went shopping in Paris. They were more interested in inventing outdoor games than spending hours in the shops. Murshid and Amina Begum, on the other hand, were enjoying their shopping sprees and thrilled to acquire furniture for their home. They were delighted to purchase a bedroom set which matched the golden parquet floor in their bedroom. The large cupboard in bird's-eye maple with a beveled mirror was very impressive. The drawers had brass handles and the mirror above was splashed on top with flowery brass decorations.

Noor was overjoyed when Amina Begum allowed her to choose a wallpaper for her own room which she shared with Claire. Murshid, too, gave his daughters a big surprise when he brought home a bedroom set in dark mahogany for their bedroom. Amina Begum then turned her attention to the Oriental Room to make it look stately. She chose white marble for the floor the same as in her salon, but she added a large mirror on the main wall, reaching up to the ceiling. The walls were painted yellow, but before it could be fully transformed into French regal style, Murshid was called to duty away from Paris for lecturing assignments.

His first stop was at Switzerland, then he went to Italy, visiting Rome and Florence. From there he traveled to England to give lectures at Bournemouth and Southampton. In England he contracted pneumonia but didn't tell Amina Begum and kept sending her cheerful letters while trying to gain back his health. He was even inspired to write poetry while on the road to recovery. One of those which he mailed to her she loved and cherished beyond expression.

To my Sharda
As pure as the water
Of a gentle stream
As near and dear
As milk and cream
As sweet as the honeycomb
As sacred as the Church of Rome
As pretty as the flower
Of Lover's dream

In response, Amina Begum sent her own inspirational bouquet of flowers.

As brilliant as the Sun
With its rays of gold
As kind as thy name
Buddha had foretold
As sacred as the mosque
With incense divine
As beautiful as stars
In the heavens shine
As holy as the shrine
Given thou in pride
Pure as the chosen one
The Rasul prophesied

Fazal Manzil was fragrant with the scent of joy and music once again as Murshid returned home. He was grateful to dive into the ocean of love from the hearts of his Beloved and beloved children. He was happy to see that Summer School in his absence had acquired more students and was flourishing. The new Lecture Hall on the Sufi Estate was complete, and he had arrived in time to participate in its inauguration. He was spending more time with his children. They were growing up fast and mature enough to tell him that they could not help missing him when he was away, and that they wished he would stay at Fazal Manzil forever. Amina Begum, of course, was always grateful whenever Murshid could spend more time with her and the children at Fazal Manzil. And this year she proudly told her Daya that Noor was the youngest poet laureate as she had dubbed her so, in Fazal Manzil. Noor had turned eleven and had written a beautiful poem.

Modest and honest
Pretty little violet
Who casts her lovely perfume
In my small garden
Come bring bright shiny sunbeams
To rejoice our happy home
Give each child their sweetest dreams
Then amidst sweet fairies roam
Than go to the poor shanty
To gladden each weary heart
Where everyone is hungry
Put on the table a tart

Predictable as ever, the happiest of reunion times were fading once again inside the jungle of duties far from home. Murshid was invited to the US once again, booked for lectures on Sufism and theosophy. As usual sweet parting with the clouds of sadness hovering above and Amina Begum exacting a promise from him that he would soon return to Paris—Home.

Once the doors of the heart are open
The feeling of humility awakens
Finding oneself face to face
With the Divine Presence
The Living God within
~Hazrat Inayat Khan

Amina Begum was constantly worried about Murshid when he was away. Especially now since he had stayed the longest in the US and was scheduled to visit Europe before returning to Suresnes. To allay her fears, he had posted her letters from every place if he stayed there more than a week. From New York he sent her a letter, telling her that he visited the Rockefeller Institute. He was invited there by a kind host Dr. Carrel who was curious to know about supernatural powers. Murshid told him that there is a power, but he calls it a natural power. Then Dr. Carrel proposed another question: Is it possible for a mystic to lift a pen by the power of thought? To which Murshid responded, nothing is impossible, but why should a mystic strive to lift a pen when by his power he can lift the heart of man to a higher ideal.

San Francisco was Murshid's favorite city and Amina Begum felt nostalgic after reading each little detail that her Daya sent her about his work and progress. He wrote that the Sufi Movement under the guidance of Murshida Rabia was alive and expanding. Reading about his lectures at Oakland and Berkley and at Paul Elders Gallery made her giddy with longing to be a part of his experience in teaching. He presided over the ceremony of the foundations for a new Khankah where mureeds can gather to meditate collectively. It was to be built on large, sprawling grounds, beyond which loomed a large rock which the mureeds named Pir Dahan. In Detroit Murshid met with Henry Ford who presented him with a model T Ford as a gift. The Detroit Newspaper next morning came up with this caption. *A Mystic and a Magnate Meet!* Henry Ford praised Murshid, saying, "I think you are preaching a gospel that men of all faith can understand. No matter what form it takes in doctrine, it is the thing Americans need."

Amina Begum received a birthday poem from Murshid which he wrote from the Waldorf-Astoria Hotel before leaving New York.

My very own Heart,

You must know that your favorable attitude would help me immensely to carry my burden which at present is too heavy for my strength. I told you before leaving Paris that I did not feel up to it. However, let us see how it works out. I would love to be home for your Birthday but am not sure if my Europe schedule would lend me the sweet pleasure of being with you. So might as well send you a Birthday poem in advance.

You will cherish my love
And long you will live
My many shortcomings
You'll always forgive
Have we not much suffered
And did we not play
Let us then continue
Being happy and gay
Stand with strength and courage
With me in my strife
Be forever my Sharda
My sweet little wife
Our little children
Always we shall love
Raising our hands we will ask
Blessings from above
Inayat with Love

Under some spell of joy and sadness Amina Begum sent him her own poem.

O purest heart ever born
Selfless and blameless
May Allah's crown adorn
Thy head most gracious

Yes, we have suffered much
But with love's sweet joy
And soon with Allah's clutch
All grief we will destroy
Life's difficult pilgrimage
Was play, with thou near
But now strength and courage
From me disappear
From Sharda to Daya

Farzal Manzil was efflorescent with joys and music once again now that Murshid had returned home after a lengthy period of absence. Amina Begum was glowing with joy, watching the little ones—not little anymore, to be educated by their father and entertained by his experiences in America. So vividly he described his visits to Los Angeles, Beverly Hills and San Diego that Noor and Vilayat thought they had seen all those place as if they themselves had visited. The mureeds, too, were eager to learn about America. They were especially fascinated by the description of a new Sufi Retreat called Kaaba Allah near Fairfax California.

Kaaba Allah was a serene abode, attracting new mureeds and blessing the old mureeds with mystical experiences. One of those who had such experiences was Samuel Lewis. He was afflicted with depression, but one evening was miraculously uplifted while meditating. Samuel was moved to tears while relating his experience to Murshid. He said in his deep state of mediation he came face to face with Khidr—Green Invisible Knight—Guide of the Muslims. Khidr guided him to a place where he saw all prophets, including Prophet Muhammad.

The dining room with its gleaming tiled fireplace had become Amina Begum's hearth of love where she sat with Murshid, sharing meals with the mureeds. They would sit there till late, talking about the wisdom of the Sufis and the mystics. Their conversations mostly enhanced by music and laughter, they sat enjoying each other's company much like a big, happy family getting together over dinner. There was so much joy and warmth of love during those late sessions that Amina Begum had begun to think, How it could be possible for any human being to have such abundance of love in such a short period of time and space. And yet she knew she was overwhelmed with joy and love reaching to such great heights that she didn't even notice the flight of time. New Year and new beginning, then spring and summer since Murshid had returned to Suresnes.

It was almost the end of summer and Madame Egeling was preparing for the Summer School to be closed for the season. Vilayat had turned ten and Murshid was planning a special ceremony for his son's initiation into Sufism. Prior to that he had received a letter from Venice requesting his presence at the Sufi Center and he had not yet made his decision to accept this invitation. He had also received several letters from India inviting him to give lectures on Sufism and his experiences in Europe and America. He was indecisive when to leave to visit his homeland.

Murshid's priority was to discuss with Amina Begum the plans for this ceremony which he was planning for Vilayat. He had even written to Murshida Rabia in America if she could come to be a part of this auspicious occasion. Vilayat was to be appointed as the Head of the Sufi Movement, that much was clear to Amina Begum. But what she was not clear about was the significance of this ceremony. She had overheard from one of his brothers that Murshids chose their successors when they felt their end was near. So, when Murshid took her into confidence about this ceremony, her heart thundered with such violence that she knew that Murshid was soon to leave this world. And when he requested that she make a yellow robe for Vilayat's ceremony, she declined his request for the first time since their marriage, hoping that she could avert the edict of fate by not complying with his request.

Murshid listened to Amina Begum's fears with a heavy heart, consoling her with so much love and tenderness that she knew this ceremony could not be postponed much like the fates which could not be averted. She helped prepare meals for the ceremony and made necessary arrangements for all the mureeds to attend and participate. Part of the ceremony was to lay a foundation stone in front of the Lecture Hall for a temple to be built which would be named L'Universelle.

The day for the much-anticipated ceremony arrived too soon for Amina Begum, but she seemed calm and composed. First the foundation stone for the L'Universelle was laid right across from the Lecture Hall in the late afternoon. A tall candle was lit by the foundation stone, symbolizing the magic wand which would help dreams come true for the devotees. Then the Sufi Garden in the back of the Fazal Manzil was where the Murshid's family and mureeds had gathered for the formal ceremony of ten-year-old Vilayat Khan to be chosen as the Head of the confraternity of the Message. Amina Begum was standing by Murshid in her blue sari trimmed with gold. Murshid stood welcoming four Murshidas, Murshida Fazal Mai, Murshida Goodenough, Murshida Greene, and Murshida Rabia who had recently arrived at Suresnes from America. Murshid announced that since there was no Murshid here, his son Vilayat Khan was to be initiated to be trained as a future Murshid as the Head of the Sufi Order.

Murshid had blessed Vilayat by laying both his hands over his head while praying silently. Amina Begum was proud of her son, receiving the blessings of his father as a teacher and Sufi mystic gracefully, but for some strange reason she could feel a cold slab of ice against the warmth of her heart. Prayers were chanted by the mureeds and felicitations offered, but Amina Begum was aware only of her son and of her husband. Even Noor, Claire, and Hidayat were lost in the background. Vilayat was dressed in a sailor suit and Murshid put a yellow sash around his neck, asking him to lead the procession of the mureeds toward the front of the Fazal Manzil. Before the procession started, Murshid removed the Sufi emblem of heart with wings from his own neck and hung it around the neck of Vilayat. A subtle fragrance pervaded the garden and the pulse of love touched every heart as they headed toward the front of Fazal Manzil in anticipation of a sumptuous dinner.

Amina Begum was still in a daze while the guests enjoyed the generous feast. She wouldn't leave the side of Murshid as if he was about to vanish amidst this river of joyful friends and mureeds. Everyone enjoyed the Indian Cuisine and the conversations flowed smooth, but sadness had settled in the very heart of Fazal Manzil. Amina Begum felt that the chill in her heart had exploded forth to envelop all in cold drafts. Murshid also felt it, but he didn't want to say anything, lest Amina Begum be frightened. Soon the guests were leaving so he bid them farewell.

After all the guests left, Murshid and his family retired to the Oriental Room. The large mirror on the white marble mantelpiece reflected Murshid holding Amina Begum close to him, his arm around her waist. Gently he turned, gathering Rubies Four in the warmth of his gaze.

"My children. This very day I Pir-O-Murshid, your father bestows upon your mother the title of Pirani, meaning the wife of Pir. I want you as well as the future generations know that your Amma is the first and the only Pirani of your Abba's Sufi Message of Love, Beauty and Harmony. You are never to forget as long as you live. And it is your most sacred duty to make sure this historical ceremony which you have witnessed, shall never be forgotten. Now come, sweet children, congratulate your Amma on this very special occasion of her being Pirani, and receive her blessings."

Noor, Vilayat, Hidayat, and Claire went one by one to kiss their mother, offer their felicitations, and receive her blessings. Then they were given leave to go to their bedrooms. After they left, Murshid held her tight in his arms, kissing and murmuring.

"Without your unceasing help, day and night, my Sharda, it never would have been possible to have brought the Sufi Message to the Western World."

1926-1927 ~ Pirani Without Pir-O-Murshid

O death, come take me by the hand
Then lay me at Beloved's feet
And with the dust my form secrete
There let me rest
~Pirani

A subtle twilight of sadness had settled in Fazal Manzil since Murshid left for Venice. He had also accepted the invitation from India but promised Pirani that he would return soon after visiting his homeland. Pirani held on to that promise after he left, but she had not ever felt so lonely, even during many of his long absences as she felt this time, mostly because she couldn't dispel the feeling of foreboding. Even the children felt sadder than before, and the mureeds walked gently in prayerful silence.

He had gone only a couple of months and it seemed like eons had elapsed since he left Suresnes. Pirani's only consolation was in his letters in which he tried to infuse humor to cheer her up along with his promises of speedy return. Another consolation of hers was that he was accompanied by Nekbakht's sister Kismet. Both were devoted mureeds and good at taking notes. Kismet had volunteered to travel with Murshid while Nekbakht stayed back in Fazal Manzil. The latest letter which Pirani received from her Daya was laden with the burden of hectic schedule, but he ended it with a subtle humor.

My very own Sharda,

My prayers arose as a burning incense and entered into the sky. In heaven they all had great ecstasy. Thoughts were moved to cry. The Lord awoke from his deep slumber and said, "I will grant you all you ask. "
Humbly lowering my head to the ground I said, "God, make easy my task."
Give my love to my brothers, also keep some for yourself.
With hearty blessings,

Inayat Khan

Pirani tried her best to be cheerful to dispel the sadness of her children, but succeeded only with the younger ones, though Vilayat could not be deceived. Noor being more sensitive and perceptive knew of her mother's sadness as well of her younger siblings but had the courage to devise means to keep all entertained. She started writing, staging and directing plays again in which all brothers and sisters could participate together for the sole pleasure of entertaining their mother. Noor as a director didn't exempt herself from acting and made everyone rehearse diligently, including herself. Then the Rubies Four were ready to perform and they performed in the living room with the mureeds as their audience and of course their mother, making her laugh with tears of joy and pride.

Noor didn't tell her mother, but she became an unobtrusive witness to her mother's deep sorrow. It happened one night when she couldn't sleep and opened her window for the night air, but what she received made her shiver with sadness. Down below she could see the lone figure as her mother pacing in the Sufi Garden and she thought she could even catch her sorrow from the cold stars under moonlit night. Since Noor was very close to Vilayat, she told him about the loneliness of their mother, both opening their own hearts how they missed their father. Vilayat suggested that they practice together to give music concerts like his father and uncles, and Rubies Four emerged as the future musicians in the living room of Fazal Manzil.

Pirani loved the music concerts of her Rubies Four and kept up the ritual of inviting the mureeds to dinners. She had also started managing activities of the Summer School with great devotion. Murshida Fazal Mai presided over the meditation sessions, but she was becoming reclusive. Mostly, she kept herself secluded in her salon or stayed upstairs behind closed doors in the bedroom suite. She used to participate in discussions with the mureeds in the absence of Murshid, but this time she seemed to be enveloped by melancholia. After mediation sessions when everyone was gone, she could be seen in a state of prayerful silence, her lips moving without sound, as if she was trying to avert some misfortune unforeseen. Meanwhile Pirani had received another letter from Murshid.

My Heart,

I am leaving Venice, getting on board on my way to India. It seems there are more houses here than human beings. Every house is built in Moorish style, very oriental, but it is damp everywhere. I would never live here for anything. This place is beautiful to pass through.
With all my love, longing to hold you in my arms.
Goodbye for now, my Sharda
Your Daya

A couple of months later, Pirani received only a telegram.

Arrived safe in Karachi, will write.

This was the last letter and last telegram Pirani had received from her beloved Daya. As months marched past, Pirani agonized in private over his health and whereabouts. Outwardly, she looked calm, going about her work quietly and trying to be cheerful. Always a loving mother, she was attentive to her Rubies Four, also keeping a close watch in preparation of dinners for the mureeds and participating in the spiritual discussions. No one could tell, yet inwardly she was wading through a stormy ocean, trying to reach her beloved through mediations, but encountering only cold mists and dark shadows barely visible. She even thought of writing a letter and sending it to his old address in Baroda, India but couldn't muster up enough strength to write. Her thoughts were pulling her back in time when she was in utter despair and had found his Baroda address and had succeeded in communicating. And yet, she was young then, hope was her dear companion, and now, a nagging presage was paralyzing her very thoughts and intuition. She could not write a word to her Daya, but inspiration was pouring out from the very pores of her hopeless, helpless pain in pearls of poesy, as if her soul itself was trying to dispel her fears and loneliness.

Come back to the soul that is dying
Without the warmth of thy love
Come back to the heart that is sighing
Beloved, for thee above

Come back to the eyes that are weeping
Blood-stained tears of despair
Come back to the lips that are speaking
Only, thy name in prayer

Pirani had written this poem as if awakening to the stark realization of her living torment that it had almost been a year since her Daya left Suresnes. The very next day she received a telegram from Kismet that Murshid was very ill in the Tilak Lodge, just north of Delhi's Red Fort in India. Just short of collapsing with grief, Pirani fell to her knees, praying and weeping. That's how Murshida Fazal Mai found her, she already knew and tried to console her with words of encouragement. Concealing her own pain and shock, Murshida Fazal Mai told Pirani that soon Murshid would recover his health and would return home, but she was inconsolable beyond hope or promises. When the children heard the news of their father's illness, they were so numb with grief that they couldn't even cry or say anything.

Noor and Vilayat hugged each other, and Hidayat and Claire joined, all four huddled together while Murshida Fazal Mai helped Pirani to her bedroom. Clinging to each other, Rubies Four went to their mother's room, now weeping in silence and praying with her for the health of their father. Sucking her own tears back, Pirani bid good night to her children, and they left with heavy hearts, only to be huddled together again in Noor's room for comfort and solace.

Left alone and with fresh surge of grief, Pirani's eyes rained rivers of torment. She felt drowned in the deluge of her own pain, blind, her very heart groping for light and serenity. Her hands were reaching out for cold paper and pen by the command of her feverish thoughts to drain out her living torment lest she die before gathering strength to pray for the health and long life of her Daya. Her eyes were raining tears, but her words were spilling fire and brimstone, black and scalding.

Can this be true or I am tossed by a snare
That findeth its way from a dreaded nightmare
A year passeth by without once a gleam
Of my adored one, O heart of love supreme

Tell me, I pray, have I lived upon this earth
Under these darkened clouds, weary of my birth
Ah, dare I to weep again, wet tears refuse to fall
I cannot speak. Aye my lips are closed to all

Finally, the gentle hand of sleep cradled her in its loving arms as her whole body turned into a prayer of supplication.

The same gentle hand which had cradled Pirani to sleep had also lulled the Rubies Four in Noor's bedroom. Close to dawn, Hidayat was jolted awake, hearing his father's voice clear as the wind-chimes. In return he was shaking Noor to a rude awakening.

Can you hear Abba, Noor? Listen, he is saying: Babuli, look after the little ones.

Noor put her arms around Hidayat, soothing him like a loving mother, blinking away her own tears. They both were falling asleep once again, adjacent to Claire and Vilayat.

***

Pirani didn't know that she had overslept, but she was awakened by one harsh blow by another telegram that Murshid had died suddenly.

Had Pirani been tossed from one nightmarish reality to another, she would not have felt such stabbing, lacerating pain as she felt now in throes of shock and agony. Her whole body felt sore, raw and burning as if it was lowered over a pyre of flames and being shredded in tiny balls of hot coals to be tossed into a conflagration of pain and torment. The cry in her heart swollen to raging deeps, exploded in one muted clap of thunder of agony and ripped through the sky before she was enveloped into a blanket of oblivion. She could feel the sharp blade of knife inside her soul, carving fresh wounds beyond imagination.

Engulfed by complete darkness, she could see the lips of her raw wound part slightly, drumming a sense of betrayal into the ears of her heart.

You have betrayed me, Daya. Why would you die and leave me alone in this world of grief and suffering?

Her winged heart was lit by the fire of rage and rebellion so profoundly insane that she thought she was dying, her body whirling over the seas and the continents to reach her beloved. Her anguished heart was caught in a litany of protests.

Why, why? You betrayed me. You said you loved me; we would never be separated.

Gleaming in its own realm of dark despair her own beloved Daya, his voice calm, his lips trembling.

Be not anxious, my Sharda
On His service I must go
Though parting is hard to bear
But it's God who wants it so

Pirani was caught in the loving arms of Pir-O-Murshid, the bliss in oblivion her love and refuge.

How long did Pirani stay in the bliss of oblivion, who took care of her Rubies Four, she didn't know. Weeks had slipped into months until she regained some semblance of strength amidst the oceans of her love and loss. Noor being the eldest, overcoming her own grief, tried to console her mother and became a mother to her younger siblings. The Mureeds attempted to console Pirani, too, but felt helpless. Murshida Fazal Mai became a pillar of support for Pirani who tended her during her illness with utmost devotion. She also sought the help of Madame Egeling in organizing a group of mureeds who would provide funds for the needs of Murshid's family with no constraints and with utmost generosity, making sure the funds were never depleted. Pirani's initial sense of rage and betrayal was replaced by depression so profound that when alone she could not contain the agony of her thundering heart within and wept inconsolably. Those were times when her body would be racked by fits of weeping and sobbing, and her sleep would move away to continents far where her beloved was buried.

Murshid had died Feb 5, 1927 and it was almost the end of spring when Kismet returned from India. Pirani clung to her like a reed whipped by the stormy waters of grief and disconsolation. She wanted to know everything about Murshid's journey, his work, his illness and his final days over the bridge of life and death. After the children went to bed, Pirani would invite Kismet into her bedroom and both would talk for hours, more so Kismet while Pirani would try to absorb all in an attempt to journey with her Beloved to the nether lands of peace and darkness.

From Karachi Murshid had traveled to Lahore on his way to Delhi. As soon as he had reached Delhi, his former followers came in throngs to greet their Pir-O-Murshid. He was lodged in the Tilak Lodge and without any time for rest, was engaged right away in delivering lectures about Sufism. Overwhelmed with long hours of lectures and teaching, he didn't realize that exhaustion from traveling and very little time for sleep was sapping his strength on the verge of a breakdown. Soon he was compelled to notice the symptoms of his fatigue when he tried to write letters during the nights, but didn't succeed, feeling week mentally and physically. In the mornings he seemed to ignore those symptoms and would brace himself to fulfill his duty in teaching and spreading the message of God Realization. In that state of low energy and weakness mounting, he kept going, first to Lucknow, then to Benares, Agra and Sikandara. Wherever he went, droves of people came to see him, and he conversed with them and answered their questions. No sooner did he reach Ajmer that he fell ill, feeling giddy and feverish. Not even fully recovered from this illness, he went to Jaipur and was anxious to go to Baroda to see his ancestral home.

Kismet had tears in her eyes when she told Pirani that Murshid felt devastated in finding his grandfather's house in a derelict condition, paint peeling off, and the gardens wild and unkempt. Pirani in return wept silently when Kismet told her that sitting on the dilapidated steps of his ancestral home, Murshid wanted to write a letter, but then sighed, saying, "I can't write to my Sharda in such sadness. I will write to Pirani when I am feeling better, a cheerful note which would make her happy. This is her home, too. She has been here in spirit, writing to my family when we were separated oceans apart, since her brother didn't want us to get married."

Murshid then visited the grave of his grandfather and returned to Delhi to rest in the Tilak Lodge. Next day he became critically ill and lost consciousness. The day after he passed away in his bed at the Tilak

Lodge, never recovering from his comatose state though a team of doctors tried to revive him, injecting medicines with hope and prayers. Murshid's followers came in droves again to attend his funeral. He was buried at the site of the Sufi Dargah of Hazrat Nizamuddin.

After Murshid's death, Kismet found in his possessions a letter which one of his uncles had written to him even before he reached India. This letter was a living proof that Murshid had been feeling ill all the time during his travels from Karachi to Baroda and back to Delhi. But most of the time he had succeeded in concealing this fact from his friends and followers. Kismet didn't know what Murshid wrote to his uncle Allaudin Pathan who lived in Nepal, but his uncle's response to Murshid clearly indicated that he had been suffering silently and patiently during his travels in his homeland. The letter below explained much to Pirani she had been wanting to know.

My dear Inayat Khan,

I am so pleased to receive your letter, but at the same time much grieved to hear you are not well and you are under treatment. Anyhow pray, let me know about your trouble and I will try my best to consult with the Baidwas here if they can give me some advice and suggest some medicine for you. I have already applied for leave. In the meantime, please let me know about your health so that I may fly and see you soon, and we may by the Grace of God, go together to Baroda. Your auntie tells me that if she had wings, she would fly at once to nurse you.

Now, my dearest one, we sincerely pray God for your quick recovery, and may God listen to our united prayer to see each other as soon as possible and give you very long life and prosperity and happiness.

May God bless you.
Your most affectionate and loving uncle,
M. Pathan

Pirani was finally awakening to the pain in living. Kismet had comforted and consoled her on the road to slow recovery. Meanwhile Murshida Fazal Mai had taken the family of Murshid under her wings, feeling passionately that it was her duty to take care of Pirani and her children. Her concern, rather generosity, was extended to Murshid's brothers and cousin also, though Mahboob Khan the older was already married and living independently, but the younger Musharaf Khan and cousin Mohammad Ali still lived at Fazal Manzil. So, she started making plans for the whole family to go to India to pay homage to the memory of their Murshid, as brother, father, husband. Pirani was grateful to Fazal Mai for her kindness and generosity and looking forward to feel being close to her beloved even if it was to kiss the dust of his homeland. She had forgotten about her birthday, but on the eve of her birthday Noor had left a poem under her pillow as a gift from her father in absentia. The very gesture of her daughter's profound love had opened Pirani's old wounds again of love lost and grief inconsolable. Rivers of tears were let loose from her eyes once again and she had to seek the comfort of pen and paper as her night companions to drain her living torment in a tear-soaked bucket of words.

O Beloved in all these fourteen years
Never did a birthday bring such bitter tears
Without thee or thy poem afar
To heal my heart from wounds that leave their soot
But now instead thou sent, thy daughter fair
At early morn, beneath my tangled hair
She lay a poem, as from thee of yore
A gift unearned from thy Jewels Four
From this day on never could I conceive
Of any birthday gift from friend receive
For what is left to celebrate for me
Since I am less than naught away from thee

Somewhat consoled after draining her sorrow, Pirani struggled to close her wounds and resume her duties of taking care of her children. Sorrow would never leave her, she knew, but she was becoming aware of her children's sadness' and activities. One month after her own birthday and four months since Murshid's death was Claire's birthday. She decided to have a special meal prepared for her and wrote a poem to commemorate her eighth birthday.

Khair-un-Nissa, so sweet and fair

With hazel eyes and auburn hair
Abba's in heaven this birthday
But he will always lead your way
He seems to be far but he is near
And to our hearts is ever dear
Yes, he will guide you from above
Just with his magic and love
To all around you sunshine give
Blest by Abba, long may you live
Amma

Claire was so happy to receive that poem as a birthday gift that she read it every night as if it was her lullaby to make her sleep comfortably. Pirani didn't know about that, but she noticed a great change in Claire as if the cloud of sadness was lifted from her young shoulders, bathing her in the sunshine of fresh hope and innocence. Pirani was spending more time with her children and Vilayat's birthday was fast approaching, just two weeks away from Claire's. She wrote another poem.

Vilayat, your Father's eldest son
Eleven years old this day
Continue the Message He has begun
His image may you portray
And may each year disclose to you
More and more your privileged life
Forget not, to Him, all praise is due
He sacrificed all in strife
He will ever guide you from above
Through all your tasks most arduous
Inspiring you with his deepest love
Long life be yours victorious
Amma

Not satisfied with what she had written, Pirani wrote another one, leaving the first one for her own solitary perusal.

One early morn, Allah sent down

A baby boy, Abba to crown
Eleven years ago this day
Carried by a glittering ray
But now Abba has flown above
And with His guiding hand of love
He holds a torch that you may see
The way that leads to purity
What birthday gift more wonderful
Than Abba's chair most worshipful
Naught so high this world can give
Blest by Abba, long may you live
Amma

A couple of months since Vilayat's birthday and now it was Hidayat's Big Ten, so she penned another poem to celebrate her second son's birthday.

Hidayat, your Father's worthy son
Just ten years of age this day
You with your brother in unison
Will spread the Message I pray
    Your sacred duty you will fulfil
Value more precious than gold
Your great heritage by Allah's will
Son of a Father foretold
    May your life be showered with success
All praise to Him, you will give
He sowed the seeds for your happiness
Long years of peace may you live
Amma

Two weeks later Noor graduated from school. Pirani felt alone and nostalgic but wanted to embellish her daughter's success with her own poetic inspiration. She was missing her Daya and wishing he could see his beautiful daughter. Suddenly, her soul was lit by the fire of love and her thoughts were spilling words of admiration.

Noor-un-Nissa, your father's pride
Modes gentle and qualified
Graceful in manner, fair of face
Worthiest daughter by Allah's grace
Deep in thoughts and wise in speech
Little comrades in school you'll teach
Today first prize you do receive
In music, highest to achieve
Tis He, who sent it from above
To His child with deepest love
~Amma

Pirani was somehow enveloped by the mists of delusion that Murshid might materialize by some stroke of Divine Power but was awakening to the pangs of harsh realization that her children's beloved father would never return to Suresnes. She was also becoming aware of the air of dissent amongst the mureeds, even of the restlessness of the Murshid's brothers. Murshida Fazal Mai was keeping all in check, though mureeds had their own ideas how to run the Summer School; Murshid's brothers wanting to dictate their own version of how the Sufi Message should be interpreted. With great patience, Murshida Fazal Mai continued to work in creating and maintaining an atmosphere of harmony at Fazal Manzil. She began to seek Pirani's help in matters of the Sufi Movement to keep Murshid's message of love afloat in Europe and America.

The wound of loss and loneliness in Pirani's heart was not healed, yet she was succeeding in keeping the rivers of agony within her contained and concealed. She was deeply grateful to Murshida Fazal Mai for planning their trip to India. In gratitude and spirit of earnest effort, Pirani decided to share the burden of Murshida Fazal Mai in Sufi Teaching and participating actively in music sessions and Sufi discussions. Meanwhile, the trip to India was being finalized and Pirani had started compiling her book of poetry, writing as foreword.

Each thought and word and line and verse
This wee book doth contain

Burst from this bleeding heart, I nurse
In loneliness and pain
Midst the blood gushing forth, I heard
Thou sayest, take the pen
And my hand, thou guideth onward
To the end, Lord, Amen

Oh! Happy days of poverty
Why didst thou flee
Giving place to the treasure tree
That bringeth misery
~Pirani

Fazal Manzil was Pirani's treasure trove, now run smoothly by Murshida Fazal Mai. There was abundance of everything, food was plenty, Sufi Movement was flourishing and the prospect of trip to India was nearing completion. New Year arrived too soon with Noor turning fourteen and Pirani wrote another poem to celebrate her daughter's birthday.

A bud from the stem of Divinity
With petals eager to unfold
To the fullness of God's vast beauty
A lovely Sufi rose foretold
With a heart full of loving forgiveness
And mind from the highest abode
An inspired soul of saintliness
With talents lavishly bestowed
Endowed with heavenly inheritance
From a Father of rarest birth
His arms surrounding you in guidance
Through many happy years on earth
~Amma

Murshida Fazal Mai's unceasing efforts in planning the trip to India was finally materialized nine months after Noor's birthday. Pirani, along with her Rubies Four and Murshid's two brothers and cousin, were soon to leave for India to visit the final abode of Murshid. For Pirani this was a pilgrimage to love lost, and for the two older children Noor and Vilayat, sadness inexpressible. The younger ones, Hidayat and Claire, were fascinated by the prospect of this long journey. In their innocence, they thought they were going to visit their father somewhere from where he could not return to Suresnes.

Murshida Fazal Mai was the sole author of arranging this expensive and extensive trip to India with generous donations from the mureeds, though Murshid's brothers and cousin pooled in as much as they could afford. Pirani was feeling sad, knowing that she was embarking on a pilgrimage to an alien land where her beloved lay interned with no promise of holding her in his arms as he often wrote and wished. Noor, being the eldest and more sensitive than her younger siblings, could sense her mother's sadness. Concealing her own sadness, she was already planning in her head how to keep her mother healthy and cheerful on this long journey.

This trip started on a foggy October morning on a ship teeming with passengers. Murshid's family had quite a few trunks and boxes since they were a family of eight. Pirani, Rubies Four, Mahboob Khan, Musharaf Khan, and Mohammad Ali. They were to travel to England to board a steamer which was run by the Cunard Line. During this journey from France to England Pirani stayed in her cabin and Noor kept her company. Her uncles and their cousin and her brothers and sister had meals on the deck and made friends with the crew and the passengers.

In London they boarded a large vessel called Rawalpindi for a long journey of few weeks to reach the shores of India. This was the saddest journey Pirani had ever embarked upon and she could barely contain her grief so as not to disturb her beloved daughter Noor. Noor was trying her best to keep her mother entertained with poems, stories, and with little anecdotes. Pirani was profoundly touched by the love of her daughter and very grateful to Murshid's brothers and cousin who had taken charge of the younger kids since they were curious to explore the ship and to feel the adventure of the sea journey. In the evenings they would run down to their mother's cabin, telling her about their escapades and saying how delicious turtle soup was and also the magic meal. The magic meal, it turned out to be, poached eggs with spinach secretly transported to the dinner table without the help of the waiters.

The ship stopped at Aden for a few hours, and Noor went up on the deck to find out about the cause of the great uproar. She was fascinated by what she saw on the deck, so vast and rather slippery. A fancy masquerade ball it was, music blaring and people drinking and laughing. Returning to the cabin, she described every little detail to her mother, even imitating a few dancers and succeeding in bringing a wan smile on the lips of her mother.

Noor would urge her mother to go up on the deck for fresh air, but she would always gently and lovingly decline. The rest of the journey, astonishing as it was, passed quickly for mother and daughter. They would spend their time reading and writing or hugging each other or falling asleep in sheer exhaustion against the burden of unspoken grief or staying awake, watching the starlit sky through the portholes in absolute awe and silence. The moon suspended in the distance was getting fuller and brighter every night. It was also getting lower as the ship approached closer to India.

Pirani was under the spell of the moon, entranced by the moonlit nights, the brilliant blue in her eyes reaching down to the shimmering silver in the ocean. When the ship inched its way closer to the Indian shore, the white moon suddenly turned to deep yellow.

"Doesn't the moon look like a lantern, darling?" Pirani murmured, hugging Noor, her heart leaping beyond the galaxies.

"Yes," Noor murmured back. Holding the poetic stars in her mother's eyes with mute reverence. Her own poetic spirit restless and throbbing.

Pirani, though sad and exhausted, was relieved to set foot on the soil of Delhi. She was welcomed by Murshid's family and friends. The whole family was lodged in a big hotel. One spacious room was fixed for Pirani and Rubies Four and another one for Murshid's brothers and cousin. They had barely settled down when Pirani, standing by an open drawer in the room, burst into a flood of tears. She was immediately surrounded by her children, all trying their best to comfort their mother. Noor was the first one to notice in her mother's hand the passport of her father.

A sad coincidence that Murshid must have stayed in the same hotel in the same room. And after more than a year after his death, his passport was still left undisturbed to be found by his beloved wife. From then on Pirani's conduit of grief was exposed to all present for she couldn't control her tears. While visiting Murshid's grave—the Dargah on the western side of Delhi, one close friend of his explained that this plot was donated by a Sufi friend by the name of Pir Nizami. Standing by the unmarked grave of her beloved, raw wounds in Pirani's heart had begun to bleed afresh. She fell on her knees, hugging the grave and crying bitterly, her stifled sobs more heartrending than her flood of tears.

The children were in utter shock, their young hearts thundering. They were unable to move or speak, watching their mother weep under a spell of misery and helplessness. Family and friends, too, were caught in a cold draft, frozen in their spots and spellbound by this naked grief of a young woman they didn't know how to console.

Pirani finally eased herself up straight, her tear-streaked face glowing with the fire of anguish. She wiped her tears with her sleeves and held out her arms to her children. The Rubies Four were swept into her loving embrace, weeping along with her. Family and friends stirred and offered them their words of comfort and condolence. Then they helped the bereaved family gently to the car and drove them back to the hotel.

Murshid's brothers and cousin arranged a tour of India for Pirani and the children before they returned to France. Dr. Allaudin Pathan, Murshid's uncle whose letter Kismet had shown to Pirani, also came from Nepal. He accompanied them on the tour and became favorite of all the children. Pirani was gratefully touched by his spirit of kindness, hospitality and generosity. At times, she seemed to be floating in mists, not really seeing, but drifting in and out of dreams. Noor was in raptures over Taj Mahal, almost moved to tears by its marble beauty, so pure and glorious. The Red Fort was another marvel where Rubies Four roamed wide-eyed, awed by the mirror palaces and floral motifs on the walls and the ceilings embedded with precious jewels.

In between the tours when Pirani wanted to rest in her room, Dr. Allaudin Pathan took the children on a shopping spree in the bazaars. He would buy them sweets and their favorite appetizer, a beetle leaf stuffed with sweet condiments. Claire loved this exotic treat the most because it made her lips red and moist. A rare trip to one coconut orchard was greatly enjoyed by Vilayat and Hidayat since it brought back the nostalgic memories of their childhood and the thrill to climb the trees in the back of their home Fazal Manzil. In this orchard they had a chance to watch one turbaned boy climb up the tree with the skill of a gymnast. He was quick to sever the coconuts from the branches, then climb down and

run away without even claiming his prized fruit. The guides were happy
to claim the fallen coconuts, break them open, and let the children taste
the milk and eat the fresh pieces of coconut.

Noor didn't want to go anywhere when Pirani stayed in her room,
but quite a few times Pirani succeeded in coaxing her to go, and when
she did, she was fascinated by the hustle and bustle in the bazaars. She
didn't want anything, but Uncle Pathan as she called him, bought for her
and Claire the bangles, earrings, and necklaces, all colorful and glittering.
He asked Noor to choose silk saris for Pirani because he didn't know
what colors she liked. For Hidayat and Vilayat he purchased paper
lanterns. Pirani went for morning walks with Uncle Pathan and with the
children. When she was tired, Uncle Pathan would drive, or they would
ride a tonga — the horse-drawn carriage. Once they took a train ride from
Agra to Delhi and found the journey most uncomfortable since it was
crowded and the people were scrambling for seats, carrying loads of
luggage.

Pirani was most impressed by the Dargah of one famous Sufi Saint by
the name of Moiuuddin Chishti in Ajmer. This site was teeming with
pilgrims of all faiths who had come to pray and pay homage in
remembrance of his saintly character. Uncle Pathan bought colorful
strings for the whole family, showing them how to tie one string each to
the marble screen. He told them to make a secret wish while tying the
string since the natives believe that the Saint fulfils everyone's wish
unconditionally. After they left, Ajmer they went to Baroda to stay in the
ancestral home of Murshid's grandfather.

Most of the rooms in this house were left in utter neglect, but Uncle
Pathan had hired extra staff and servants to make this house hospitable
for the family of Murshid. Pirani was in a daze as if her Daya would
suddenly appear and she would be swept into his arms magically. Much
like the time when she had lost him in America and through his family in
Baroda, she was able to be reunited with him in Europe. Much of the time
she spent on the balcony in contemplative silence, watching a stream of
people going to work or running errands. Sometimes Noor sat with
Parini on the balcony, but sensing her mother's need for privacy, she
went down with her brothers and sister to play in the garden. Their

uncles kept them busy with improvised games of skipping rope or playing the sport of cricket.

One evening Pirani sat meditating on the balcony but was conscious of her children's voices who were playing down in the big parlor. In her meditative state, she thought she heard Murshid singing, his sweet voice fluttering up from the street down below. Jolted to sudden awareness, she looked down and could see her Daya strumming his sitar as if poised to serenade. She couldn't move, but her voice was loud and clear as she sought the attention of her children down below.

"Your Abba is back, sweet children. Go quickly. Take wet towels. He is standing on the street and sweating,"' Pirani sang with joy.

All children raced out of the house as if whipped by the currents of a hurricane. Hidayat being the fastest was the first one to land on the street. All four were doused with the waters of disappointment as soon as they encountered the deserted street with the exception of a couple of women sweeping the front steps of their house and talking. Raising their eyes to the balcony, Rubies Four could see their mother standing transfixed, her gaze blank, she seemed oblivious to her surroundings.

During the last few weeks of their stay in India before they left for France, Pirani, though attentive to the needs of her children, appeared to be suspended under a spell. Noor was old enough to know her mother suffered against the clouds of her own delusion and daydreaming. She was witness to her mother's claim, insisting that she could hear her Daya singing over the balcony at night and in all her waking, sleeping hours in this house of his grandfather. Pirani told Noor that she could even feel the presence of Murshid's grandfather, enveloping her in the warmth of his own love to mitigate her pain and longing.

It had almost been three months since they came to India and the day they were leaving it was the cusp of spring. As a parting song to her Daya, Pirani bid farewell to Baroda with a poem in her diary.

India knowest thou, God hath blest
Thee with his diadem
Ah! Tis hidden far within thy breast
Form all who could contemn
But to ye that seeketh truth above

Disclosed is the hiding place
Lo! Tis sparkling rays that bring light and love
To all with God's own grace

The journey from India to France was another painful passage of time for Pirani. The farther the ship advanced, the farther her beloved was left behind in continents apart from Europe. Noor, as usual, kept her mother company while her brothers and sister mostly stayed on the deck with their uncles. At times Vilayat would come down, trying to coax his mother and sister to come on the deck to watch the night sky sprinkled with a myriad of stars. Pirani always declined, but Noor sometimes ventured to go up on the deck with her brother Vilayat. One cold night while looking at the sky she told Vilayat, "These cold, glittering stars up there fill my heart with sadness profound and nameless."

Noor was content to stay with her mother, both entertained each other with a treasure-trove of stories, or with their poetic inspirations. Also, they could read for hours and get so absorbed in their books that they would forget to eat their meals. One evening Noor delighted her mother with a new poem she had written a night before. Pirani was pleasantly surprised to discover that her daughter, in her early teens, could create such a masterpiece of inspiration. She complimented Noor on her talent and perception, telling her that her poetry could move even the great poets to tears of joy and ecstasy.

Beloved, ah, beloved Amma
A treasure stored deep in our heart
Tis flowers of our gratitude
A treasure that never will depart
Behold, for their petals are carved
With Allah's own heavenly art
Their beauty on the longed for day
To you and Abba we impart
Through life's struggle and through life's strife
May we treasure as our life's gem
The seed in our heart you had sown
Ah! Quote in the sacred Nirtan

And always remember this
The path of the heart is thorny
Which leads in the end to bliss

Th bleak and long journey was nearing its end. Pirani looked sad and forlorn, her heart longing for bliss which she knew she could never attain. Her anguished thoughts were lit to inspiration and she spilled those on paper. Noor watched her scribble hastily and Pirani could not help sharing it with her beloved daughter.

Mightier than the breakers of a stormy sea
Dashing on the rocks till a pieces be
Why then cannot this, mine anguish for thee
Break open these walls hiding thee from me

One day short of reaching the shore of France, Pirani wrote another poem while Noor had gone on the deck with her brothers and sister.

Guiding star of my life
Where art thou soaring
Far from thy earthly strife
Through heavens alluring
How came thee to depart
From Sharda, thy love
Didst thou not know her heart
O heavenly dove
Come, hear her soul weeping
For thou who hast fled
In despair she is seeking
Her grave with the dead

1929-1930 ~ Sufi Movement at Suresnes

Every weary night as I lay me down
The lovely image with flowers I crown
And the blessed shoes that thou hast worn
Are kissed by the tear-stained eyes forlorn
~Pirani

Fazal Manzil didn't feel the same after the death of Murshid. After returning home, Pirani was enveloped in clouds of depression. The Oriental Room was locked to preserve the memory of beloved Murshid, more so to avoid the painful recollections. Mahboob Khan became Murshid's first successor to continue the tradition of Sufi Movement of Pir-O-Murshid, Hazrat Inayat Khan. Madame Egeling kept alive the tradition of Sunday Service in the Sufi Summer School. Several devoted mureeds still came to the Fazal Manzil for Universal Prayer Service and actively participated in spreading the message of Sufism under the guidance of Murshida Fazal Mai.

Amongst the Rubies Four after returning home, Noor was the first one to notice that the Quince tree under which her father used to sit was dead and shriveled. She dared not tell her mother who was already reliving her grief in a dark pool of silence and reflection. Pirani and Noor had become closer to each other than ever before, sharing their grief and poetry and their quiet moments of solitude. Noor was transferred to a secondary school at the Lyc'ee de Jeunes Filles in St. Cloud. She was studying French, English, German and Literature. Pirani spent more and more time alone in her room. She wept often, wrote poetry, and couldn't forget the land where her beloved was lost forever.

Far across the seas to the land divine
Where mystery reigns supreme
God carrieth there each thought of mine
And every wondrous dream
Under the warm Sun, in a golden tomb
Resteth thy beloved form

Midst the fragrant rose that round thee bloom
Sheltered from the wind and storm
With unceasing peace for many an age
O holy one, thou art blest
Numberless souls to pay thee homage
And kneel at thy feet to rest

This poem above was written during one of those nights when her pain of loneliness had uncurled like the serpent of torment. At the same time a realization had dawned upon her that soon it would be the second anniversary of her beloved Daya's death, his first one lost in the ocean of her grief. This painful realization had jolted her, reminding her with a harsh blow of guilt that her children needed her love and guidance. Noor had been her companion in pain and loneliness, but Pirani had neglected Vilayat, Hidayat, and Claire who were being cared by the uncles and the mureeds. Mureeds, too, were Murshid's children, Pirani thought with a pang of sadness, and she needed to pay attention to their inner growth of purity in living and the kernels of spirituality. Awakening from under the spell of inertia and depression, Pirani set to work to commemorate the death anniversary of Murshid. But before commencing that giant task, she sat down to finish her poem, The Pilgrimage, which she had started writing during her journey from India to France.

Ocean of love, O sympathetic sea
To thee I bow in humility
For thine own compassion carrieth me
To the land of my dreams, my life's safety
O India, land of splendor divine
Salutations flow from this heart of mine
Whilst I enter thy border of mosque and shrine
And trod over this sacred soil of thine
Delhi, my Delhi, so richly inlaid
With a priceless jewel from God that strayed
To illuminate souls that have watched and prayed
Aye o'er all mankind, its rays hath sprayed
Thro' scenes of wonder I roam at far, in quest

Speechless and breathless, of the world divest
With eyes cast downward, I kneel to be blest
At the foot of the sweetest rose strewn nest

The doors of the Oriental Room were thrown open. Pirani gathered her Rubies Four to help clean and restore it to its former purity and brilliance. All the carpets and the furniture were to be taken out, and Noor and Vilayat were eager to be the chief helpers. Hidayat and Claire were assigned the task of carrying the pails of water and cleaning with mop and broom. Pirani brought in a large bucket containing floor polish and steel wool pads and copper polish. Fazal Manzil was infused with the pulse of excitement as the whole family worked together with great passion and hearty sense of devotion.

All the windows were washed with water and vinegar and scrubbed dry with the old newspapers. The furniture was dusted, and the chairs and tables polished to a smooth sheen. Some chairs with inlay of ivory and mother-of-pearl were carefully and meticulously cleaned. All the handmade Indian shawls to cover the screens were aired out under the Sun. Even the walls were dusted and the large mirror over the mantelpiece rubbed with muslin to perfect brilliance. There were quite a few pieces of bric-a-brac of glass which were washed with cold water, and the ones of brass and copper were polished. When all the things were put back in the Oriental room, Pirani had breathed a sigh of relief, complimenting her children and hugging them lovingly and gratefully.

On the day of Murshid's death anniversary, Pirani got up in the early hours of the dawn. She made a fresh wreath of yellow roses to hang it above the photo of Murshid over the white marble mantelpiece. She lit incense in all corners of the Oriental Room and assigned her children the responsibility of greeting the mureeds. Murshid's golden shoes were placed on a chair along with two silk tea-colored roses made by Madame Egeling. There was a continual stream of mureeds entering the Oriental Room, carrying bouquets of roses which they laid at the foot of the chair paying homage to the memory of their beloved Murshid.

During this long day of mureeds streaming in and out, Pirani retired to her bedroom to rest whenever she felt tired while Rubies Four greeted each guest pleasantly and tirelessly. Most probably Pirani wept in her bedroom when she went there on the pretext of rest, for when she would return to the Oriental Room, the red streaks in her blue eyes could not be mistaken for the fire of rubies and sapphires, but ridges of grief unslaked.

As the evening descended, Pirani sat with a few of the devoted mureeds at the dinner table and with her children who had greeted all day with patience and with the spirit of dedication. After the dinner, they all went back to the Oriental Room for prayers and a few moments of silence. After that, Pirani gave her speech of gratitude which she had written weeks in advance.

Most devoted mureeds of our beloved Pir-O-Murshid,

I am grateful to have the privilege of conveying to you a few heartfelt thoughts on this blessed day and ever living day as we unite in this sacred ceremony in prayer and remembrance. Thoughts that are so simple are so very true, for truth lies in simplicity. Was not our Master simple, yet so deep?

May our hearts dictate to us the true and simple object of the Summer School. Is it not to unite us all in love, beauty and harmony, which is our Master's message and which alone will spread the message over the whole world? Thereby we fulfil the sacred duty to our Master, proving our devotion to him and in doing so we purify our hearts, which alone allow our souls to receive the light for which we are striving, that we may see through the darkness of the earth.

As our Master has helped us in the past, to purify our hearts and to make our minds clear, that we may have right understanding. Even so is he helping us and will continue helping us until our hearts become pure enough to receive the light which is the aim of our life, our eternal goal.

We have but to think in our Master's words. Allow our actions to be guided by his words and our speech controlled by his words. Then only we are his true devotees, and then only can we spread his message in the world.

I wish to express to you our deepest appreciation for all the help given to us, prompted by the sacred thought of your love and devotion for our Master.

With blessings from Above

Life at Fazal Manzil without the Murshid was sad indeed for Pirani, except for a few slivers of joys when her children entertained her with their music or when she accompanied them to the concerts. Music was the children's gift of love from their father, and for Pirani, sacred consolation in remembrance of her Daya. Kismet was an angel lending great help, encouraging the children to play music, paying for their musical education, and introducing them to the best singers, musicians and composers of Paris. She enrolled all Rubies Four in the music school l'Ecole Normale de Musique under the guidance of Nadia Boulanger.

Noor began studying how to play harp, so Pirani bought her a golden harp from the Erard. It had small wood carvings of two dogs at its base, for protection. Vilayat was learning how to play cello, Hidayat the violin, and Claire the piano. Kismet often took all children to the newly built Concert Hall Salle Pleyel where they could meet the famous masters behind the stage. This was a double treat for the children since being able to come to this new Concert Hall itself was a great privilege. Behind the stage, they got to meet Segovia: Casals, Heifetz, Ezenberg, Marian Anderson, and Rubenstein. When alone, Pirani enjoyed playing the piano. And when she could she went to the concerts, her favorites were the music of Messenet, Opera Thais, Song Berceuse, and the Tales of Hoffman.

Such blissful nourishments of the soul were few and far between the hardships, Pirani was suffering under the weight of burden both emotional and financial. Murshida Fazal Mai was the only financier of family needs left in the Fazal Manzil since most of the mureeds had left to live in Paris. The ones left behind had stopped contributing toward the maintenance of the household of Murshid. The only one to help Pirani in household work was one concierge, Madame Codonnie, who dusted and cleaned or helped with the ironing.

Pirani was cooking for the children and for the mureeds, too, at times, not letting her impoverished state add more sadness to her Rubies Four than they already felt in the absence of their father. When her hands were sore and her knuckles bleeding due to washing, she decided to write to her uncle George Baker for funds to meet the expenses. Her uncle lived in New Mexico and was a wealthy lawyer as well as owner of a cattle ranch and was delighted for the opportunity to help his niece whom he remembered as a young girl of great beauty and intellect.

The generosity of Pirani's uncle lessened the worries of financial constraints, but other worries concerning the spiritual wellbeing of the mureeds didn't diminish. She had been noticing after coming back from India that slowly and gradually most of the mureeds had begun to hide themselves in their own shells of aloofness. Soon, she discovered to the chagrin of her own perception, that they were jealous of each other, rather critical, and dogmatic. Their minds had become like a clockwork of control machines as to who was best suited to be the guardian of the Sufi Message. Even the brothers of Murshid were afflicted with a feverish drive to exert their control over the children. Pirani had to step in to save her Rubies Four from the harsh punishments which their father would have never approved for any child. Some of the mureeds were getting belligerent, too, amongst themselves, and a few of them becoming possessive of the children, so Pirani once again had to be strong and assertive to make sure that her children were never subjected to negative influence from any source.

Another spring without Murshid and Pirani had almost succeeded in keeping her children as comfortable as possible. In fact, Noor was the pillar of her health and strength behind her own shield of resolve and earnestness. Now, Vilayat was joining Noor in sharing the responsibility of being a father to his younger sister and brother as Noor had been a mother to them when Pirani had suffered bouts of illness and depression after the death of their father.

No illness or depression visited Pirani this spring day, for it was Easter Sunday and she was grateful that her Rubies Four were blossoming more beautiful than the spring flowers. She could inhale the fragrance of white carnations in the garden below from her bedroom window. She felt comforted, as if feeling the presence of her Daya in the very shadows of Fazal Manzil and its gardens. Standing close to the window and looking down, her gaze was arrested to Murshid's favorite pear tree now in full bloom. It seemed as if her Daya was somewhere in the garden, walking barefoot over the dew-drenched lawn, each little dewdrop shining like a diamond against the shafts of early sunlight. Yellow blooms of acacia stood sparkling and pansies and crocuses appeared to lift their heads up to the shuddering disc of a sun mirroring the earth.

Noor and Vilayat had already planned for Claire and Hidayat an Easter goody hunt in the garden. Pirani kept standing by the window, recalling yesterday's activities in cooking and planning. She had gone shopping with the intention of buying meats and vegetables to cook a special meal for the mureeds who would be bringing cakes and flowers as they had done every year even after the death of Murshid. But instead of buying what she intended, she had settled for cheeses, baguettes, and fresh dairy milk. The luncheon for the family and mureeds was already prepared a day before with the help of Noor, and cheeses were cut into cubes to be shared with the neighbors.

Before the Easter hunt, Murshida Fazal Mai conducted the Easter Service in the Reception Room which was darkened by drawing the curtains. The electric lights were switched on, highlighting a large table with a yellow tablecloth. This table was hosting several candelabras and all holy books of the major religions, the book of Sufism placed in the center. Murshida Fazal Mai lit the candles and read a sermon which seemed very long to Claire and Hidayat.

As soon as the sermon was over, the Rubies Four marched out into the garden, Claire and Hidayat eager to find out what Easter Bunny had brought for them. Before finding anything, Claire was overjoyed to espy the little Robin perched on the same branch as it was seen sitting a year before one Easter Sunday. Soon she cheerfully gathered home-colored eggs from the windowsills and from under the bushes. Hidayat, too, found quite a few eggs and little foil-wrapped candy hidden in the flower beds. Pirani was happy to see her children enjoying this beautiful spring day and thinking about the promise of rebirth which Easter conveys.

In the evening after supper when Pirani said goodnight to her Rubies Four, Noor could not help noticing shadows of profound sadness in her mother's eyes. She, too, was sad and missing her father. She went to her room thinking that Fazal Manzil itself was mourning the loss of her father, and as soon as she reached her room a quatrain poured out of her sad heart on a piece of paper as she sat at her desk trying not to weep. With a heavy heart she got up and plodded toward her mother's bedroom, but finding the door closed, she slipped the folded piece of paper with quatrain sealed within through the crack underneath.

Pirani read the quatrain and wept quietly, her heart reaching out to her beloved daughter with love and blessings.

Lo! His thoughts so deep
In sparks are manifest
To console your heart
Throughout life's painful test
Noor

Hugging her daughter's gift of consolation to her heart, Pirani snatched her own pen and paper to drain her sorrow in hope of a bright tomorrow.

Oft' times methinks it cannot be
That thou shall never return
With heavy heart I wait for thee
And watch and pray and yearn
If thou shouldst come from the dead
And Lo! Thy form I meet
Never would I raise my aching head
From off thy blessed feet

Tears were welling into Pirani's eyes and so were beads of inspiration in her tormented thoughts as her fingers moved feverishly in an effort to still the pain of loneliness.

I know not why this strength is in these bones
Nor why beats this bleeding heart
How does this earthly form live through its groans
Alas, since thou didst depart
Tis a mystery hidden from my sight
But lo, with the tide of time
My fiery love, itself shall light
The candle of truth sublime

Oh Lord, once more to see thy face so sweet
No sacrifice would I spare
Just once to throw myself before thy feet
God of mercy grant my prayer

1931-1939 ~ Burial of Grief Before Big Storm

This poem Abba has written
To console your heart
His thoughts through his dear children
To you he doth impart
~Noor

Pirani had succeeded in burying her grief, sloughing off her mantle of depression, and suddenly coming face to face with this stark realization that her children needed her loving care and encouragement for success and inspiration. She was glad to notice that the Summer School at Suresnes was gaining more students, and that the mureeds were becoming active inside the circle of Sufi Movement. They were still possessive of Murshid's children, but they were becoming very helpful. Murshida Fazal Mai was ageing quickly, but still able to conduct the Universal Worship Services. Murshid's brother Mahboob, along with his wife Shadi, had moved to Holland a year ago, and now his younger brother Musharaf Khan followed his brother, taking along with him his cousin Mohammad Ali. Madame Egeling had taken charge once again, keeping the household running like clockwork and keeping account of all the needs of the family and of their expenses.

Fazal Manzil was coming alive with music after four years of Murshid's death, his children following in his footsteps. The Rubies Four had turned out to be great musicians, giving concerts in the Oriental Room at home and in the Concert Halls of Paris. Noor had become proficient in playing the harp and the piano. Vilayat played the cello and the piano, but he preferred cello. Hidayat, more passionate about music, loved to play both piano and violin. Claire was hooked on piano and was as good as her older sister and brothers. Occasionally, even Pirani accompanied her children on the piano. As a young girl growing up in America, Pirani had played guitar, but after coming to Europe she didn't think of having one or playing, yet, now her interest was awakening. She told about this to Kismet who now was not only her friend, but confidante. She went with Pirani to all the concerts when the children performed.

Time had literally streamed past on winged flight, leaving behind one year and marching hurriedly. Pirani was amazed to acknowledge that her children were not in their early teens anymore except for Claire. Pirani could remember when Noor was sixteen and infatuated with the son of one of the mureeds. That boy had asked for her hand in marriage from Mahboob Khan who had vehemently rejected the boy's proposal on the grounds that his niece was much too accomplished to marry a young man who didn't have good education. Noor had accepted this decision of her uncle without making any fuss since knowing that her mother didn't approve of this match either. So, as a token of reconciliation, she wrote a poem for the sole comfort of her mother.

How oft throughout life's puzzling path
Our feet have gone astray
Ah! Dear Amma you will forgive
Our endless faults this day

Pirani mentored as well as encouraged Noor to write poetry and short stories, especially for the children. Noor proved to be a fast learner. She became so proficient in writing children stories that she even earned a prestigious Baccalaure'at Certificate from her school Lyc'ee de Jeunes filles. Pirani was proud and grateful that all her children were exceptionally talented. Vilayat, only sixteen, had started taking interest in reading lectures of his father with the intent of being active in the Sufi Movement. The Sufi Center had all the writings left by Murshid, so they handed stacks of papers to Vilayat to study and contemplate. He literally took it to heart and was very passionate about studying the works of his father. The first thing he did was to purchase a giant oak bookcase which was placed in the dining room, and the dining table became his big desk to read his father's writings and the works of the ancient Sufis. During this intensive schedule of reading he even started writing a spiritual drama titled The Light of Truth.

Hidayat was not to be left behind, rather inspired to write poetry. A year earlier, barely fourteen, he had fallen in love with a pretty girl and wooed her with poems, sharing one with his mother. How the affair ended, Pirani couldn't recall, but she remembered the poem he had written.

My heart yearns for you
Do you not know, my beloved
That a heart yearns for you
In the ocean of your beauty
This yearning heart drowns
Do you know, O my dear one
That to yearn everyday
Is a pleasure that rejoices me
And exalts me with love

It was heartwarming to Pirani to watch her poet son Hidayat turn to a skillful electrician. He had picked up this hobby a few months ago and had fixed all the faulty connections in Fazal Manzil. While testing his new skills, he had even succeeded in adding new fixtures for Vilayat in the dining room with extra lights so that his brother didn't have to tax his sight with poor lighting.

For Pirani, Paris was becoming more like a reflection of her own thoughts, much like her unspoken thoughts about her Rubies Four whom she envisioned as the beautiful notes on the piano of life. Another year had flown past and it was time for the Dutch Baroness Agnes Sophia Van Pallanett to perform her annual ritual of visiting Fazal Manzil, her Sufi name was Sarojini. She had become Pirani's close friend after the death of Murshid and in his loving memory loved to spoil his children. Each year when she came, she brought expensive gifts for the children and then took them shopping, treating them like royalty. Without fail she would take Noor and Claire to exclusive shops in Paris and buy them summer dresses from their favorite shops Le Printemps and Gulries Lafayette. Vilayat and Hidayat were equally spoiled by her, buying stylish shorts and expensive shirts. At times the boys soiled their fine clothes while indulging in rough sport of homemade hockey in their garden, much to the chagrin of their mother, but Sarojini would laugh and persuade Pirani not to reprimand the boys. Noor, always sensitive to her mother's feelings, would write poems on behalf of Rubies Four to cheer up Pirani.

> To our Amma,
> See your little ones
> Unfold in your heart's bright ray
> As buds with teardrops bedewed
> Unfold at the dawn of day
> Even if the whole world
> Would save us and help us even
> Still it could not equal
> Your tender motherly care
> Forgive us, dear Amma
> For often we lose our way
> How oft in this world
> You keep us from going astray
> Hidden within our hearts
> In deep gratitude for you
> May it bloom more and more
> For none can be so true
> Lo! His thoughts so deep
> In sparks are manifest
> To console your heart
> Throughout life's painful test
> Ah! Beloved Amma
> Ever keep this before your eyes
> My sorrow forget not
> Once again joy will arise

Besides writing poetry and studying music, Noor had joined Sorbonne University of Paris to study child psychology. Pirani encouraged Noor in this new field of study, also complimenting her on her writing since she kept adding more children stories to her large collection. What Pirani could not encourage was the frequent visits of one of Noor's friends at Fazal Manzil. His name was Goldberg and he was a fellow student from her music class at the Ecole Normale de Musique. Pirani did not particularly dislike him, but he didn't seem to fit in with the whole family. The Mureeds, on the contrary, after discovering that he wanted to marry Noor, made their dislike known, expressing their disapproval that Pirzadi—the daughter of eminent Pir-O-Murshid could not marry beneath her class. This didn't deter Goldberg from visiting and Pirani, being a gracious hostess, couldn't tell him to leave, moreover she didn't want to hurt the feelings of her beloved daughter who liked his company.

***

Years were trailing after years and another year was left behind. Pirani was glad to hear from the old friends of Murshid from Holland, Sirdar and his wife Saida whose real name was Baroness Tuyll. The Baroness and her husband invited them to spend a few weeks with them in Holland. Pirani was grateful of this invitation, thinking that her children would have the opportunity of expressing themselves freely once away from the regimental schedule at Suresnes.

Holland turned out to be a bucolic retreat and the children were overjoyed. Saida took Noor and Claire under her wings, teaching them horse riding. Pirani was comfortable with horses since as a young girl she went riding with her father in America. Now in Holland, she was eager to get up early and go riding in the morning. Soon Vilayat and Hidayat followed her example and joined her. Barely a week since they came to Holland, Rubies Four had become proficient riders. Noor had mastered the skill perfectly and her prowess was challenged by Vilayat, Hidayat, and Claire in a competition and as expected Noor was the winner.

Pirani, for the first time after six years of Murshid's passing, had been able to suppress her pangs of grief, feeling a whiff of joy in riding and watching her children enjoying themselves. Noor was not only riding horses but riding on the clouds of inspiration. Saida had touched the chord of Noor's inspiration, recognizing her talents as an artist and an accomplished horse-rider. After discovering that Noor was a writer and had translated Buddhist Jakarta tales from Hindi to French, Saida suggested that Noor should translate her stories from French to English.

Noor had told Saida that out of five hundred of Jakarta tales, she had translated quite a few which were stories and fables about the previous incarnations of Buddha. Saida was greatly impressed, promising Noor that she would help her publish the Jakarta tales and she herself would do the illustrations. Noor was ecstatic, her young heart filled with gratitude and overflowing with love when Saida surprised her by renting a harp so that she could play in the evenings.

Noor was not the only one getting special treatment, Vilayat was beneficiary of great attention from Sirdar who wanted to guide the young initiate on the path to Sufism and Sufi activities. They would sit in the library for hours, talking about the ancient Sufis and their works. Hidayat, too, would keep his brother company, eager to learn and enjoy all male companionship.

Saida was a gracious hostess as well as generous and delightfully entertaining. She would take Pirani and the girls to other Dutch towns to watch summer events or simply explore the beauty of Holland. In Leiden, Pirani enjoyed the flower exhibition. So great was her joy that she wouldn't tire of saying that she had not seen such fabulous floral arrangements ever before in her entire life, not even in America. Time was drawing close for the family to return to Suresnes and Noor was feeling a little sad and nostalgic. Noor had become so close to Saida that she shared her diary with her since Saida wanted to know more about Murshid. Saida's heart was filled with tenderness for Noor more than ever before after reading this entry in her diary.

The first lesson Abba taught to his little ones was to open their eyes to selfless love and devotion and constant sacrifice of their Amma. He painted in our little hearts the ideal of motherhood in all its beauty and purity. Heaven lies at the feet of the mother, he told us, this saying of the Prophet. He taught us to show our gratitude in the smallest little way, to renounce gladly to a game or amusement if we saw the least little thing which we could do to give joy to our Amma, or if we felt that our playing caused her the least displeasure. When playtime was over before the night covered our solitary house in the fields, the little ones went off to sleep. Most of the time Abba would hold Claire in his lap and tell us stories of his childhood. He would tell us of his love for his mother and the sweet deeds which that love brought about. He rooted in our souls the feeling that our first and most sacred duty was towards our mother, and even our prayers to God were secondary. For the prayers of the child who does not consider feelings of his or her mother are not heard by God.

Before saying farewell to Holland, Pirani requested Noor to share her song with the kind host and the hostess. Noor had written this song a couple of years ago and it was Pirani's favorite. This special song was titled Madzub, dedicated to the sages of the East.

At thy feet, O Madzub, I came to seek rest
In the fire of thy glance may this yearning soul be blessed
Thy footprints of crushed thorns are strewn with pearls divine
And lo! Their glory unveils the dazzled eyes of mine
Through life's test, may this heart, O thou living shrine
As a lotus once blooms, bloom on their rays of thine
At thy feet, O Madzub, I came to seek rest
In the fire of thy glance may this yearning soul be blessed.

That joyous time in Holland seemed a distant memory now that they were back in Fazal Manzil. A sadness was visiting Pirani's heart and once again she could feel the presence of Murshid inside the house and outside the gardens. And yet she was happy in a way to watch her Rubies Four excel in music, literature and spirituality. Especially Noor, who had also started to learn how to play veena. She was very adept in writing music compositions and had written, *Song to the Butterfly: Prelude to Harp, Elegy for Harp and Piano.* Along with her music practices and music compositions, Noor was busy translating the Buddhist Jakarta tales from her French version to English. Always fond of children, Noor had started inviting the children of the mureeds to Fazal Manzil, telling them the epic stories of Ramayana and Mahabharata.

***

Another year had flown past since their return from Holland and it was already time for Pirani's birthday. To cheer her mother, Noor wrote a birthday poem, her personal gesture of celebration.

I saw a little Birthday man
Skipping along the way
I stopped awhile and listened
To hear what he would say
He put his little finger
Upon his little head
He blew the dandelions, and
Danced around and said
Why, this is my best Birthday
For on this very day
The storks brought down a girly
Whose name is Ora Ray
I must put on my sweetest
And wear my golden crown
I'll take my happy knapsack
And wear my brand new gown
She has had cloudy hours
And many cloudy years
And many hard adventures
And many, many tears
Life has been very naughty
But I shall fight the wrong
And make the whole life happy
Just with my little song

Pirani was always comforted by Noor's sensitivity and inspiration and grateful for her cheerful disposition. But she was finding it most difficult to support her daughter in her relationship with Goldberg. Even Vilayat was not pleased with Goldberg's so-called music accomplishments or with his demeanor. The mureeds who frequented Fazal Manzil and participated in the Sufi Services or helped with the Summer School, didn't approve of Goldberg's intrusion in the house of late Murshid. Madame Egeling, who lived at Fazal Manzil and supported the family financially, also didn't approve of Goldberg. All this opposition was taking toll on Noor and she was feeling the burden of stress, though apparently remaining calm and poetically inspired. Pirani could feel her daughter's pain and confusion, struggling in vain to comfort her, facing only a stark ocean of helplessness. Astonishing as it seemed, even the stressful times had grown wings and the flight of time was a measure of two years already dissolved. Vilayat had turned twenty and Noor churned out a beautiful birthday poem for her brother.

> Just listen to what the birdies say
> That twenty years ago this day
> From heaven came a little boy
> And brought on earth a world of joy
> And long was he awaited here
> To be his father's sonny dear
> And all along the way, his love
> Will bring him blessings from above

Vilayat loved Noor and admired her talents, but he didn't trust her infatuation with Goldberg. He was growing spiritually and intellectually, rather perceptive, and sensing constant flux of tension at Fazal Manzil. Pirani, too, was feeling the burden of Goldberg's unavoidable presence against the weight of unanimous dislike for him by the mureeds. Even Noor could not avoid the fresh currents of stressful opposition, torn between her love for her mother and her attachment, rather obsession, to Goldberg's company. Vilayat, intuitive by nature, stumbled upon a notable discovery that if he could take Noor away from Fazal Manzil for a while, she would gain a clear understanding of the present constraints and would be able to end her relationship with Goldberg. He suggested that they take a trip to Switzerland. Noor assented quickly, eager to get away from the stuffy atmosphere at Fazal Manzil. Pirani was relieved, hoping that Noor and Vilayat would have a grand time in the land which her Daya called Paradise. Winged time of flight once again, one full year had flown past before their plans could be materialized to leave Suresnes. Vilayat was twenty-one now and Noor wrote a quatrain for his birthday.

> May every wish of yours come true
> And every day be clear and blue
> Of my brother dear, a man this day

May joy come along your way

Noor looked forward to this trip to Switzerland, especially with Vilayat, feeling that she and Vilayat had special affinity of friendship between them since they were children. Pirani sent them on their way with blessings and prayers for their safe return. She was hoping that Vilayat's assumption could come true that once Noor's head was cleared, she would be willing to end her relationship with Goldberg. They traveled to Geneva and Zurich, then toured the Swiss lakes and went skiing and climbing the mountains. When they went rowing on the lake of Geneva, they couldn't help but talk about their father. Blissfully experiencing the peace and beauty of this place which had inspired their father to build a Sufi Center in Geneva. They met several of the Sufi disciples, and Noor sang songs to the children of the mureeds. She confessed to Vilayat that she felt close to her father again in Switzerland. Two weeks of vacation had worked wonders on Noor's mind and body, and on the way back to Suresnes she told Vilayat her fondest memory of childhood. When she was little, her father would rock her on his knees and say.

When Abba's love is there, what fear is there?

Fazal Manzil was imbued with the light of joy and hope and positive energy after Noor and Vilayat returned from Switzerland. Pirani was happy and relieved since Noor, on her own, had formally ended her relationship with Goldberg. He had accepted Noor's decision graciously and had stopped visiting Fazal Manzil. A subtle sense of freedom had begun to seethe in Noor's psyche, and she started playing Veena again, also resumed her practice of playing the harp every evening. She had become proficient in Hindi but continued her lessons at the Ecole des Langues Orientales of Paris University. Within a year she succeeded in earning a degree in Child Psychology. Her music skills were improving as well as her skill in writing. She had picked another set of Jakarta tales for translation about the previous incarnations of Buddha. Pirani was proud and impressed by Noor's multi-talents, especially when she started writing stories for the children's page in the Sunday Le Figaro.

A full year of amazing accomplishments by Noor with the promise of more at the inception of this New Year and Pirani was glowing with joy.

Noor had established herself as a great writer, finishing translation of twenty stories from the Jakarta Tales. Her stories on children's page of the Sunday Le Figaro were being broadcasted on the Children's Hour of Radio Paris, receiving great reviews. She had started writing articles based on the Indian and Greek legends and about the women singers, one Indian poet and singer Mira Bai, another one Emma Nevada and her daughter Mignon Nevada. Prolific as she was, she wrote both in French and English, adapting French and Nordic folklore, and also wrote about the Indian emperor The Great Akbar and about Charlemagne.

While basking in joy about Noor's accomplishments, Pirani was also proud of Vilayat's spiritual success in Sufism and Hidayat's active participation in the cause of the Sufi Movement. Her youngest daughter Claire was excelling in music and studies and Pirani's heart was filled with gratitude for her blessed wealth in Rubies Four. Another jewel Pirani had embraced with all her love was Hidayat's newly wedded bride. He name was Leni, titled as Iman after her marriage. And yet much like the ship on stormy waters of the ocean, Pirani's fabric of serenity could not escape the ebb and flow of rough tides. This time it was shattered by the darkening clouds of another war, reminding her of the ravages of the First World War she had endured along with her Daya.

The reek of war was swift and abrupt, it had already reached Paris with astonishing speed, bringing in its wake dread and bewilderment. Germany had invaded Czechoslovakia, forging an alliance with Italy. Even Noor's energy and enthusiasm were deflated by this dread of war, hovering all over Europe, though her book of twenty Jarkarta Tales with illustrations by Henriette Willebeck Le Mair was published in England by George G. Harrap. Germany was emerging forth as a volcano of terror and devastation, its next invasion was Poland. The world was shocked by the power of Germany on its mission to invade the entire world. France, Australia, Great Britain and New Zealand, as allies, declared war on Germany. Pirani knew that this war was the inception of another world war and she and her Rubies Four would be sucked into its dungeon of tragedies vast and unavoidable. Panic seized her heart and she scribbled in her diary.

Before this frame is fallen

Wilt thou give it strength to stand
To carry duty's burden
Lord, that is thine own command
Before this heart is bleeding
Wilt thou nurse it with thy love
Until the hour thou chooseth
Lord, to call me there above

Pirani's former spirit of agony was yawning to an abrupt awakening
and she wrote of a desperate need to be close to her Daya.

What need had I for the light of the day
Or the moon in the night to lead the way
O Beloved when thou wert near
What need had I for the summer's warmth
Or the cooling breezes swaying forth
O Beloved when thou wert near
What need had I for a bright sunny morn
Or the shining stars, the dark sky adorn
O Beloved when thou wert near
What need had I for the showers of rain
The fruits and the flowers thou didst sustain
O Beloved when thou wert near

1939-1940 ~ Exodus to England

Oh envious world, oft thou tried in vain
To tear asunder or to put in twain
Our love, which naught but death can separate
Nay even death is left disconsolate
~Pirani

Pirani, for the first time in her life, found herself alone at Suresnes. The threat of war hovered above like thick fog over Fazal Manzil, but Noor and Vilayat were gone on a trip to Spain since they had planned this vacation months before the looming threat of war became imminent. Hidayat and his wife Iman were the first ones to leave Suresnes since they decided to move to Holland. A few days after Noor and Vilayat left for Spain, Murshida Fazal Mai wanted to take Claire with her to Holland to visit her family and friends, and Pirani, considering Murshida Fazal Mai's age and frail condition, consented. The fear of Germany invading France had scattered the mureeds in various parts of Europe in hope of safety with their families. That was how Pirani was left alone in Fazal Manzil. She missed her children, but for some astonishing reason, she was swept warmly into the soft embrace of her solitude—reading books, writing poetry and reminiscing about her journey to India. To her it was a pilgrimage of love lost and love unforgettable and she finally sanctified it on paper with profound sadness and nostalgia.

In India, land of my dreams
Ah, where my heart's vision gleams
May I be blest
Oh death, come take me by my hand
And lead me to my loved one's land
From life distressed
Alas, for thee, long years I weep
O sing me peacefully to sleep
Gently caressed
Then lay me at Beloved's feet

And with the dust, my form secrete
There let me rest

The threat of war was drawing close and Pirani had begun to worry about Claire's safety and about Murshida Fazal Mai who had grown old and feeble. Hidayat and Iman were in her thoughts, too, but she knew they were well settled in Holland. Hopeful and prayerful as always, she would pray for the safe return of Noor and Vilayat while seeking the company of pen and paper to scatter her worries or journey back in time over the bridge of memories, her passage back to France from India.

Hearken! The gong of duty's call, alas
The hour of farewell has come to pass
But this heart is left buried beneath the grass
Nourished by fragrant soil, beyond surpass
These eyes are dim with tears, this head bent low
These lips refuse to utter thoughts that flow
Through the silent air, sympathetic breezes flow
And rays of light spread forth their brilliant glow
A sacred band awaits across the sea
That dares to link this piece of clay with thee
O, thine own strength pour on a frail trustee
That mouldeth a true and worthy devotee
This life is pledged to every faithful friend
Those selfless service to our Murshid lend
Thence, in humbleness, their loving call, I tend
Storing within, this yearning till the end

End of one lone, inspiring week and Pirani got news of Murshida Fazal Mai's death. Claire wrote that Murshida Fazal Mai didn't show any symptoms of any ailment and probably didn't suffer but died in her bed peacefully. A funeral service was held for her a day later attended by family and friends. Claire had contacted Hidayat, so he and his wife with their newborn son Fazal also came, bringing along with them a group of mureeds. Claire was also able to contact uncle Musharaf and he and his wife Savitri came for the funeral, and Murshida Fazal Mai was laid to rest with prayers and great reverence. Claire ended her letter by saying that she would return home within a week, accompanied by Iman and Hidayat and of course their adorable son, Fazal. After reading Claire's letter, Pirani's old wound of grief was popped open and she cried without restraint, praying for the safe return of all her children.

Murshida Fazal Mai had died in third week of December and now New Year had descended upon Fazal Manzil wrapped in the dark shroud of warring tragedies sure to follow with all its fanfare of doom and destruction. Meanwhile, Pirani had taken a short course in helping the mental patients, remembering the agony of the veterans in deep depression after WW1, and now she wanted to be ready to help if her help was ever needed. Noor and Vilayat had returned from Spain, so did Claire with Aman and Hidayat and Fazal from Holland, also uncle Musharaf and his wife Savitri with their newborn son. Claire didn't get a chance to contact her uncle Mahboob in Holland and regretted leaving without seeing him and his wife, but Pirani consoled her that in such times of warring threats it was better that they stay safe wherever they were instead of venture traveling. She was also thinking about the safety of France as a whole and suggested that Claire and Noor get trained for nursing in case their help was needed on the front in the event if Germany decided to invade France. Noor and Claire registered for a six-month training—an intense training course in Red Cross Nursing School. Considering the vulnerability of Suresnes directly exposed to German Attack, Hidayat believed they move to South of France, but Vilayat was hoping to explore possibilities to move to England since they were British Citizens.

Pirani's world was shattering once again after gaining a semblance of peace for a few years. She was afraid for the safety of her children amidst the frenzy of another world war. The King of Belgium had abdicated, and Belgium had already capitulated to Germany. Now that the Germany had declared war on Paris, most of the Parisians were fleeing to South of France or to Spain. Panic and confusion were settling in the heart of France and rumors were floating around that any British subject residing in France would either be killed or imprisoned. Vilayat, being the head of the family, decided that he would arrange for the whole family to move to England.

Noor and Claire had recently graduated from the Nursing School, and Vilayat had masterminded the plan as to how they were to move to England. The whole family was saddened beyond words, especially the girls when they heard from Vilayat that if Germany invaded France, Fazal Manzil would probably be occupied by the Germans. All was in order, Vilayat was to drive one car with Noor, Claire and his mother, and Hidayat would drive his own as a convoy, but ultimately would head toward South of France with his wife and son, thinking that he could help the Resistance better from there than staying in Suresnes. Musharaf Khan was of the same opinion and decided to move to South of France with his wife Savitri, thinking of staying close to Hidayat and his family wherever they could find good accommodation.

Fazal Manzil was left behind and Pirani was caught in a daze. She could hear guns in the distance. A smoke screen was drawn over Suresnes by the French soldiers, artificial smoke to fog out people so that they could leave safely. Vilayat's sports car, an MG, was only two-seater. Pirani sat in the front passenger seat, while Noor and Claire were squeezed in the jump seat in the back. Hidayat with his family in his own car was following but was soon lost in the pandemonium of the traffic jams, Vilayat's car barely crawling its way toward the train station.

Finally, when Vilayat made it to the train station in Tours, it was under attack, targeted by incendiary bomb which succeeded in destroying the rooftop. Pirani and the girls were frightened by the loud shattering of the enormous glass roof in a shower of icy splinters. The train was delayed, but Pirani got a chance to see her old friend from Red Cross, Mademoiselle Guerineau, who had worked for the children's social services in Paris. Mademoiselle Guerineau was also fleeing Paris, but she was an influential lady and gave Pirani a recommendation letter addressed to Mademoiselle Feitsch—the president of social services in Bordeaux. Pirani thanked her friend profusely and was very grateful. A few hours of grueling wait and the train came, Pirani with her children boarded the train toward Bordeaux. But after reaching there they were not allowed to get down as the city was overcrowded, so they had to continue their journey to a small port town of Le Verdon fifty miles north of the harbor of Bordeaux.

After reaching Le Verdon, Noor was in tears saying that she had forgotten to bring the copies of Croix Rouge — French Red Cross Nursing Certificates and insisted on going back home alone to fetch both the certificates, her own and Claire's. Pirani wouldn't allow her to go alone. Claire jumped in saying that she would go with her, but Pirani maintained her stance of refusal. Noor sounded so desperate that Vilayat appealed to his mother on her behalf, saying that they could wait for both to return, then take a ship to England. Soon he was able to convince his mother that it would be safe, so Pirani agreed reluctantly.

Claire didn't know that Noor also wanted to stop at La Rochelle, Brest on St. Nazaire to report to the British Red Cross that they were going to England. It turned out to be a journey of horror for both Noor and Claire, for they never even made it back to Fazal Manzil. It was evening when they reached the Red Cross Ship, thirsty and exhausted. Suddenly the lights went off and they were not allowed to leave till morning. Also, there were many dogfights overhead. Their only option was to return to Le Verdon. Hurdles appeared at every step and they had to change many buses and were compelled to hide in small boats until morning. Finally, they reached Le Verdon next day in the afternoon. Pirani was close to a nervous breakdown for she had heard on the radio that anyone seen on the streets in France was to be shot by the Germans.

United at last with tears of relief flowing freely from the eyes of the mother and the daughters, Vilayat urged them to hurry up and they all boarded the last cargo ship which would take them from Le Verdon France to Falmouth England. There exodus began on Vilayat's twenty-fourth birthday, but they had no means to celebrate. After three days of cramped journey, they reached Falmouth, England. Pirani decided that they go to the home of their old family friends, Basil Mitchell. The Mitchell family lived at Southampton and when they arrived there, they were most warmly welcomed by Mr. and Mrs. Mitchell. They stayed with them in utmost comfort for a couple of weeks until Mrs. Mitchell found out that Southampton could be the next target of German bombing. Mr. and Mrs. Mitchell drove them to their friend's house in Oxford to ensure the safety of the Murshid's family.

Barely had they settled at Oxford when Pirani felt the need to be self-sufficient to feed her children. She was lucky to get a job to take care of the mental patients at a nearby hospital. Vilayat, too, wanted to help, so he joined the Royal Air Force. Unfortunately, as soon as he started his training, he was afflicted with paratyphoid fever. After his recovery he was told that he couldn't join the Royal Air Force since his sight was affected by the fever, so he applied for the Royal Navy. Meanwhile, Noor and Claire had joined the British Red Cross and were assigned two weeks of intensive training in First Aid.

London was under assault, suffering the brunt of bombings by the German Luftwaffe against the British Spitfires, but Oxford was not under attack. Pirani, besides working at the mental hospital could spare some time to teach Claire sowing since they had left Fazal Manzil empty handed and needed to build their wardrobe. Noor also pilfered some time from her First Aid Training and wrote an article for an English Newspaper about her experience, rather her escape, from St. Nazaire when she was there with Claire, hoping to reach Fazal Manzil to fetch the Nursing Certificates.

"At the docks of St. Nazaire all had changed. The town was stunned stiff, wild eyes, tensed chins. Their voices seemed choked. We sat and waited for the next ferry. The dock was crowded. The news, *France on fire, in flames, Paris, gates open. The tomb of their unknown soldier guarded by the enemy.'* God, it was worse than death.

In a flash twenty generations passed through every mind. Charlemagne, Joan of Arc, Napoleon, Foch? The whole life of a man passes before him when he sees death.

Tell this to our English comrade, said one soldier. *Tell them that we will fight for it back, every acre of it. We will go to the other end of the world, but we will fight for it back.*

The will of a whole nation was poured out to the world by his quivering lips. Can the will of nation be crushed? Perhaps suppressed momentarily. Simple are those who believe that all is peace in France. Of all whom I have come in contact, not one is ready to submit. I can challenge that at this very moment, thousands are giving their lives *Pour la patrie* for their homeland. Their secret hope is Britain across the sea. We hold a task never in history a land has held before. No, France shall not die. France shall live again."

The feeling in Oxford was of hope and outward calm while the sirens wailed over London. St. Paul's Cathedral was bombed by the Germans and the news of war was a constant reminder that the whole world could be engulfed in its fire of death and devastation. The burden of fear and uncertainty was taking its toll on Pirani. She could hide her worries, but not her symptoms of fatigue and apprehension. Tears of relief welled into her eyes when Vilayat received a letter from Hidayat and he read it aloud to his mother and sisters.

Dearest Vilayat,

Since receiving your telegram from Le Verdon we have been living in anxiousness about you all. What a blessing it was for us to receive news of you through our dear friend, Mehtab. As for our journey, we left Le Tranche the day after the Armistice and drove as far as we could till it got dark and gloomy. To refresh your memory, French Prime Minister Paul Raynaud resigned, succeeded by Marshal Henri Petain'—the hero of Verdun in the First World War. Petain' initiated some sort of Armistice which was broadcasted from a radio station from the Bordeaux. The end result of which turned out to be quite depressing. To honor the treaty of Armistice, Paris and north of France and the entire coast is to be administered under the command of the German Military. A so-called free zone south of Loire is to be the French Military under the command of Marshal Petain'. His headquarters are set up in Vichy in the Auvergne. The Vichy regime, known to be sympathetic to the Germans, is assigned the task of governing the entire area. Swastika has replaced the tricolor, but enough of this.
We are now at Solignac—Haute Vienne in the Chateau Marbouty. This is a little village near Limoges. Nekbakht has returned to Suresnes to her little house on the land of Fazal Manzil. She says she has been able to transfer quite a few important things from Fazal Manzil to he own home. Fazal Manzil now is occupied by the German soldiers. We have heard that our uncles are in Hague and are well, but we know not more about them. Initially, uncle Musharaf and his wife wanted to stay close to us, but then decided to move to Hague. Please give my deepest love to the girls and to dear Amma.

Love from Hidayat

WWII had finally reached its full swing, but Pirani was too busy to notice its volcanic eruption, moving the entire horde of humanity like the defenseless rookies on giant chessboard. She was working hard, staying prayerful, yet worried and bewildered. General de Gaulle had managed to escape from France and had settled in Britain. He was broadcasting from London, rallying Free French Forces to his side and calling for continuation of Freedom Struggle. Emboldened by this Noor had started to wear the emblem of Free French—a double barred cross in silver. If this was not enough to frighten Pirani, Noor had joined the Women's Auxiliary Force to help the cause of France. She was also studying to be a radio operator.

Noor had gone to Scotland for a training to work for Women's Auxiliary Force. Vilayat had joined Navy and was stationed in London, sending little notes at times to cheer up his mother.

Dear Amma,

Our ancestor Tipu Sultan was a tiger, our Abba a lion. I am gargoyle and Noor is deer.

Pirani had moved to a small apartment in Edinburgh since Claire had enrolled in a university there to study pathology. Claire was practically living on campus, but Pirani wanted to be close to her youngest daughter. Claire was involved in researching penicillin, using agar-agar and petri dishes, making her mother proud and intrigued.

Whenever Noor got time off from her training in Scotland, she would visit her mother in Edinburgh. At times, Noor would bring a few friends, including her close friend Joan, and Pirani would lovingly serve them tea and cakes in her little apartment in Edinburgh. Sometimes Claire could also come when Noor and her friends were visiting, and Pirani enjoyed these interludes of love and warmth, shutting out the ugliness of war, at least for short periods of time. Vilayat, too, came to gladden Pirani's heart, but occasionally. While waiting for the active duty as naval officer, Vilayat had delved himself deep into studying philosophy and comparative religions.

Pirani, though still not accustomed to working long hours, was spending less time at home and more at the hospital. She could not help but miss her Rubies Four, thinking no Sun of Love ever came to light her little apartment. Fatigue and loneliness were her constant companions, but more and more she was embracing the muse of her poetry for strength and sustenance.

O shining Sun of heaven and earth
Spread forth thy brilliant rays
In thy home, there is no more mirth
Gone are the happy days
Help me to climb up the golden stairs
To the height thou mayest soar
Wiping away all sorrows and care
To kiss thy feet once more

One evening when she came back from work in her lone apartment, she felt so overwhelmed with grief and despair that she wrote this poem, barely able to contain her ocean of tears.

This bleeding heart, forlorn
Cruel fate hath tossed, until
In thousand fragments torn
Is left to suffer still
From this poor form entrapped
All life, all hope hath gone
Pale with death's garment wrapped
And yet must linger on
Descend most Holy One
And with thy helping hand
Pray, let all grief be shun
And take me to thy land

Bitter nights of despair
Hath made fragrant the air
And teardrops turned into dew
I watch and I wait
Till thou doth open the gate
And thy love leadeth me through
~Pirani

Rubies Four, circa 1939

World War II had grown into one dark giant cloud, engulfing all nations in the conflagration of its warfare. Europe was smarting under the assault of Germany and uniting hands to defeat the forces of Hitler. Meanwhile, Indians were pushing for independence from the British Imperialism. They were in favor of the war against fascism and serving side by side with the British forces to defeat Germany but wanting concessions in return for backing England. Though one politically motivated Indian of great fame and wealth, by the name of Subhas Chandra Bose, was favoring alliance with Germany to get rid of the Imperialism. A couple of more great Indian politicians, Nehru and Gandhi, had their own views in Struggle for Freedom, but were supporting England against Germany. Noor and Vilayat were the ones keeping Pirani informed of the world politics, also telling her about their own active roles in defeating Germany. Pirani was alone most of the time, staying in touch with her children through the exchange of letters. After Hidayat's one letter from France, Pirani had not heard from him, but had hope that the war would end soon and then she would get to see him and his family. Even Claire who was not far away and not actively involved in any war related activities, could not get away from work to visit her mother and when she could, only briefly. She wrote to her mother regularly, always hoping that Noor would steal some time out of her busy schedule and would be visiting their mother.

Noor in fur collar

Dear Mother and Sister Sweet,

These last two days I have been looking through the microscope from morning till afternoon. Can you imagine, we test microbes with various strains, of which Noor is very familiar. She would be proud to know that now I can handle a microscope without the help of any instructors. The glass in the Focus

Tube is believed to cost ten pounds. I have seen so many microbes that I see them all over the place now. I wish I could have a photo of myself to look through the microscope.

Love, Claire

Claire, circa 1935

Pirani's eyes would well up with tears whenever she received letters from any of her children, reading them repeatedly to feel the warmth of their nearness. Vilayat was still in London. She worried most about him since he lived in a small room in Premier House on Southampton Row in Bloomsbury. That was the place where the German planes hovered above, exploring strategic targets. Noor was in Abington under some sort of Army training, of which Pirani didn't know much about. Vilayat wrote to her mother that Noor visited him in London, but she didn't want to disclose what she was being trained for, though Pirani could guess that Noor was involved in some sort of Secret Army Mission.

A note from Noor arrived on Pirani's birthday, and she couldn't fail to notice that it came from Wiltshire. While writing back to her she wanted to know what she was doing in Wiltshire, but desisted, respecting her vow of privacy concerning her job and training. With that little note, Noor had also sent a poem to her mother which Pirani read every night, feeling the comfort of the nearness of her daughter.

> So dearest, chin up, it's your Birthday
> And all that we wished shall come true
> We are on duty but it is play-day
> And life is all just pink and blue
> And our cheers are going all over England
> Three cheers from the Bodleian Lanes
> Three cheers by wireless from Scotland
> Three cheers from the RAF Planes
> Noor

Noor visited Vilayat in London again on his twenty-fifth birthday and he wrote to his mother about this very short visit of his sister. Telling Pirani that since they both are interested in the Indian Independence Movement, Noor's Birthday present to him was an autobiography of the Indian political leader, Nehru, published in Year 1937. She also brought for him his favorite score of Bach's Toccata and Fugue in D Minor

Vilayat also sent Pirani a little note on her birthday, hoping that he would see her soon. He also wrote snippets of updates about war: Germany had attacked Greece, Bulgaria and Yugoslavia. Pirani was always grateful to receive little morsels of news about warring enormities of the Germans. Her help was needed in so many medical facilities that she was constantly tired and couldn't keep abreast with the latest invasions of Germany. Besides her worries about her children were an added strain to her fatigue since Claire had joined the Army as a secretary to the Captain in the Medical Corps in Woolwhich. Claire was working long hours, deprived of sleep and feeling the brunt of exhaustion. It had been months since Claire had last seen her mother, but a great shock was in store for her when she got some time off to visit her. She found Pirani looking frail and forlorn, cooking fish over a gas burner on the floor. This was her new apartment at Tawington Street in London and Claire didn't know up till now that it had no kitchen. Despite the impecunious circumstances, both mother and daughter were happy to be together, praying for the health of Noor, Vilayat, Hidayat and his family and for peace in the world.

Claire stayed only a few days and peace was a distant dream against the blaring of sirens. Pirani had lost count of the days and the months. Her beloved homeland, America, had also become the victim of waring absurdity. Japan had attacked Pearl Harbor. America and Britain had declared war on Japan. Vilayat was now fully active in the Navy in the service of HMS—Her Majesty's Service. Noor was fully commissioned in the Army, but never disclosed in what capacity she was working. War raged on and Pirani didn't realize that an entire year had slipped past until Noor's little poem reached her on her Birthday.

While passing the well of water
Where all the wishes come true
What wish did we make little Mother
If not for sweet little you
We wished that our toil would bring riches
That we could hand over to you
We wished and God grant wishes
To make Mother happy too
So, dearest, chins up, it's your Birthday
And all that we wished shall come true
We are on duty, but it is a play day
And life is just pink and blue

One month after her birthday Pirani got the devastating news that Paris had fallen without a struggle. The pre-war talk of dirty Germans was replaced by the German propaganda to dirty English. Paris was emptied out of all Jews. All Jews above the age of six were required to wear the yellow stars and were imprisoned in France, then sent to concentration camps in Poland and Germany. The apartments vacated by the Jews were seized by the locals and the Germans at bargain prices. Many French people were quick to collude with the Germans. The Vichy Government was so eager to please the Occupiers that it began handing over the Jewish children even before the Germans asked for their custody.

Though immersed deep in work, Pirani's past melody of depression was returning. The old wound of Daya's absence was ripped open and bleeding afresh. Sweet Absent was somewhere in her soul and psyche, trying to comfort her, but failing. She was always eager to listen to Noor's story of *The Fairy and the Hare*, on the Children Hour of BBC, but even that didn't bring her any consolation. She was missing her Daya and her Rubies Four. Paradoxically, her Daya was both absent and present, more so now than ever, since India was going through the labor pains of Freedom Struggle. The Prime Minister of Britain, Winston Churchill, had sent Sir Stafford Cripps to India to meet with the Indian Congress leaders, promising India full dominion status after the war if the Indian Congress cooperated with the Britain during this conflict with Germany. The Cripps Mission had failed, Gandhi calling it the post-dated check, urging Indians to, *Do or Die*. Nehru joined in the chorus, urging the Britain, To *Quit India*.

Churchill was remorseless, declaring, *I have not become the King's first Prime Minister in order to preside over the liquidation of the British Empire*. Pirani was aghast since hundreds of thousands of Indians were being recruited to the services of the British to fight in Italy, Africa, and in the jungles of Burma and Eastern India. How, why and when it happened, but the top Indian Congress leaders were jailed for subversion. Before Pirani could awaken from her shock and disbelief, another year had slipped past, and Noor's poem arrived for her Birthday, a respite most sad and endearing.

You see it's the loveliest day
We all have such a lot to say
Why is it tell us Mother dear
We long for this all through the year
Do you remember when quite small
We peeped behind the garden wall

To watch the birthday man pass by
And pull his bag and ask him why
We wish and if our dreams come true
And if the ones we have for you
Were in his knapsack tucked away
To give to Dearest on this day
He said that he had loads of love
And joys and presents from above
And off he went, but now we are grown
Wherever has the Weeman flown
It is up to us this time to be
The birthday man and try to see
Just how much joy and dreams come true
We will manage to make up for you
Just how much happiness we will make
Just how much time all this will take
We are apart and far away
But wasting not a single day
We want to make life a success
And toil and strive for happiness
And gain it just because there is you
So tally ho! We will carry through

With this poem Noor had sent a brief note that she was joining the Cavalry Forces for *Special Services* duties and would be gone for lengthy periods of time. She ended this note with assurance that she would write regularly. After reading this note Pirani felt an ominous prick inside the very core of her soul, her very heart raising a cry of warning that Noor would be in trouble. For the first time in her life, Pirani felt the need to dissuade her Babsy, as she called Noor, from joining those special services, so she sent her a quick note.

Dear Little Babsy,

We think of you every day and all day long. Absentmindedly I wait every night for you to come in the door. I wish you would decide to remain where you are, rather than to accept the special services duties. For I am certain you are less exposed to the trial of life for which you are not strong enough. Do consider my judgment a little bit, won't you, Babs?

Love,
Amma

Noor, in fact, had committed herself to serve as a British Secret Agent in Paris, decoding Nazi Germany messages and communicating via Morse Code with London. None of her family members knew about this. The person she said farewell to before she left London was her younger sister Claire. They met in a cafeteria at Baka Street in the underground subway station. Claire was visibly shaken after her sister left and when she reached home, she told Pirani about the brief encounter cautiously and reluctantly.

When Claire asked her where she was going, Noor responded, to British Voluntary Cavalry Force, adding quickly. "When the war is over, I shall be wearing the family tartan on horseback." Claire asked her what color that was, and Noor said, lavender. Before leaving Noor had warned Claire, "Should the War Office write to you about joining, don't do it." Then she hurried to leave, Claire following. "Don't follow me," Noor warned over her shoulders. "I have to rush. Bye bye, little Sister, be good to Amma." With dithering heart, Pirani had listened to this exchange, but didn't want to upset Claire, so she consoled her by saying that Noor will be all right. A week later, Pirani, Claire and Vilayat got letters from her, addressed individually.

Cutest Little Mother,

Such a joy to be able to post a letter to you. So much to tell you in a minute, Mother dear, how can I? How happy I was to hear about you, but just to dash home as I used to and see you. Mother cute and give you a surprise—nothing I long for more. Still it might be sooner than we think, someday, what a day! Please don't worry, girlie, when you don't receive any letters. We are not so far apart after all. I do hope, by my next leave you will have a new flat to come to, the one I am dreaming about. How I long to see Vilayat and Claire. Mother cute, I wish you would give up Red Cross work for some time. I know you are exhausting yourself and this thought keeps me constantly worried. I feel so helpless over here, not being able to look after you. Do excuse my pencil,

Mother, I can't help it. I am sending you Elizabeth Arden products I found by chance on one of my journeys. A friend of mine will bring them over to you. Another friend promised to phone, did he? I really miss you terribly, Mother. I talk to you so often in my sleep. Still, next time you see me, I will be bonny and beautifully well and shall we celebrate? With Pin and champagne! And you must be young and bonny too! That's how I am looking forward to seeing you. Cheers, dearest, a big kiss and all the love in the world.

Little Babsy

To Vilayat Noor wrote.

Brother Dearest,

Nothing could have infuriated me more than to have to leave without seeing you, just at the time when I was longing to see you the most. How are you, old boy? I am looking out for you. Maybe we will meet someday, somewhere, somehow? What a day that would be, and what a lot we would have to tell each other. How well I can picture you on the front deck in your smart blue, facing the wind with the same frown as in your little MG. And every time the Navy puts up a show, I just feel terribly proud of my brother. And duty can pull us apart at different ends of the world, but it only strengthens ties, and brother is dearer than ever. We will carry on, old boy. Wish me some luck and same to you and victory very soon. Thanks for the money you lent me for my perm before my interview for this job. Somehow I found out you didn't have any, but you borrowed money to make me happy. Tally-ho and all the love from Babuli.

Noor's letter to Claire, sharing with Pirani as Vilayat did earlier.

Girlie Sweet,

How I miss you! What a celebration when we meet again! How are you, girlie? Have you a little crown on your cap yet? Isn't it awful not receiving letters? Just knowing you are well, that's all. Still, girlie, it has taught me that wherever we go in the world, we never can find a substitute for a sister or a brother. Perhaps mine are exceptional, maybe. But, gosh, we had a lot of fun together, and my little sister makes me laugh more than anyone else. Girlie, I am so worried about Mother. Could you do something about her stopping to work at the Red Cross? It's too much for her I know. Besides, she must see a doctor for her throat. Still I will be seeing you and we will have such a lot to tell each other, and by that time you will have a wee little crown on the cap and be looking very snob. In the meantime, don't forget little Babsy completely and be good. A big kiss.

Babuli

Despite Claire's appeals, Pirani spent most of the time working at the Red Cross than resting at home. She was in a constant state of fear and anxiety about Noor and Vilayat since she didn't know where they were posted. Her only consolation was Claire, with whom she could communicate occasionally. The ravages of war were endless and heartrending. With more wounded soldiers or civilians arriving every day, Pirani worked long hours, snatching only a few hours of rest or sleep. Her only respite or luxury was when Claire visited, though staying briefly. They both would luxuriate in the warmth of nearness, listening to the Irish American singer John-McCormack on BBC Radio and feel a little consoled, shutting out the warring absurdities. Had they known Noor was in Paris as a British spy, they would have been collapsed in utter fright. As it was, they were blissfully ignorant and always felt grateful whenever they received her notes or letters. A few months after her initial letters which she had sent before leaving London, another one arrived addressed to Pirani.

Mother Dearest,

If only I could describe to you the lovely spot I am in, simply marvelous. Of course there is such a lot to do that very little time is left to contemplate the scenery. I feel I would like to bring you around here on a holiday tour after the war, who knows! How is the naughty little girl who never writes and Vilayat? Mother, please don't worry if sometimes my letters are long reaching you. You see, it is rather difficult at times being in reach of a place to post. It seems there has been some difficulty about your letters reaching me. I am afraid they have been following me around. I am so longing to receive them. Cheerio and big kiss.

Babuli

Some sort of presage had settled in Pirani's heart. Despite Noor's cheerful notes, she had a feeling that her daughter was being sucked into dark voids of danger and devastation. At least, Vilayat was back in touch, once that he had received his officer's commission in the Navy. She didn't worry much about Hidayat since as far as she knew he was not working for any Army and had a family, intuitively knowing that he would be safe. Claire still visited occasionally whenever she could spare a few hours from her work. Aside from intuition, Pirani was becoming victim of her own delusions. At times she thought this was WW I, her Daya was with her, both trying to keep baby Noor comfortable, also struggling to make sure that the Sufi Movement was alive and flourishing. This delusion itself was lending her strength, the spiritual and loving energy of Daya was with her, letting her withstand the fatigue of long hours of work and to ward off the pangs of separation from her Rubies Four. Winter was approaching fast and she received another precious morsel of news from Noor.

Dearest Little Mother,

Simply too marvelous to receive your wire! I was so happy, Mother dear, so happy! Bravo for Vilayat to get the Officer's Commission! I am afraid, Mother, the unexpected leave I was hoping for has not come. Maybe if I don't expect it, someday it might come and I just can't imagine a sweeter dream than to be able to pop home and give you a grand surprise! It's a date! Mother cute, I wish I knew some details about you. Have you been to the doctor? To the dentist? Couldn't you really make a noble effort? Busy as I am, Mother dear, I manage to go to the dentist. Please don't neglect a day longer, you do keep me worried. Had it been sooner, Mother, I could have saved two wisdom teeth, just had to be pulled out, sheer neglect. And do be good and not worry about me because I am fine, Mother dear, and looking quite bonny! And soon I will be right there with you and there will be such a lot to talk about, such a lot to celebrate! Isn't the news about Vilayat's promotion simply grand! We will be together, it won't take so long after all, will it? Do send me a wire again soon. A big kiss and just tons of love.

From little Babsy
PS: A big goodnight kiss goes over to you every night! Mother dear! It's when I miss you the most.

Pirani hugged this letter to her heart as if this was her last, knowing not that it really was, her heart already shedding tears of blood. A few days later Vilayat received a letter from Noor, and he sent it to his mother, as Pirani always loved to read Noor's letters.

Brother Dearest,

How grand to hear about your Officer's Commission, congratulations! I am so happy. I guess everything is strenuous right now, but very interesting. I miss you terribly, but realization never leaves me that the war is still raging. Is your glass of sherry ready? Mine is! We will go to Italy. Fancy, not even being able to chat about all the events with you. Brother dear, it sometimes breaks my enthusiasm.

Till we meet again, old boy, cheers and good luck and all the love in the world.

Babel

Pirani tried her best not to worry, but some sort of deep rent in her soul throbbed with a warning that Noor was in danger. Her heart was breaking with the pain of fear and separation and for solace she turned to inspiration, her poetic plea a glow of fire.

Harken, O, Angels of heaven
I beg ye each and all
Come hither with trumpets laden
To help me in my call
With challenging force together
Blow ye all trumpets you
Call him with sounds that mightier
Never was in time agone

1944-1946 ~ Great Tragedy of World War II

At the close of the day
When life's toil fades away
And all so peacefully sleep
No rest do I find
Since thou left me behind
Till death around me doth creep
~Pirani

Nightmares were visiting Pirani in her sleep as she lay on her cot in her small apartment after long hours of work at the Red Cross. Fatigue and loneliness were taking a toll on her health since Germany was gaining victories and the whole world was trying to find means to check their machinery of death and destruction. Her heart was reaching out to Noor all her waking, sleeping hours, restless and fluttering. She had not heard from Noor for several months, still hugging her last letter as her talisman of hope and reunion. Instead she had received an enigmatic note from the War Office.

Dear Mrs. Baker Inayat,

We are glad to be able to let you know that we have just received a message from your daughter. She asks us to forward her dearest greetings to you, Claire and Vilayat, with lots of love.

This little note was no consolation to Pirani, but a bullet of fear and suspicion. Her heart was a volcano of presage, telling her that Noor was in imminent danger wherever she was, otherwise she would have sent a letter in her own handwriting. The War Office had provided Pirani with an address, so she immediately sent her a letter and a can of sardines, Noor's favorite. A few months more of agonized wait and finally Pirani received another equally enigmatic typewritten message from the War Office.

Dear Mrs. Baker Inayat,

Thank you for your letter and telegram, the contents of which were passed on to your daughter. I am well pleased to tell you that she is very well and sends much love to you, Claire and Vilayat.

By this time, Pirani was in throes of hopeless, helpless pain, unable to dispel or contain this living torment of not being able to communicate directly with her daughter. Her own work at Red Cross, though strenuous and heartrending was rather a palliative to her aching heart to escape her own painful misery, for which she could find no outlet.

Due to the volcanic fury of the war, Claire was working overtime at the hospital, literally staying there, mostly deprived of rest or sleep. Vilayat was also sucked into the furnace-belly of the warfare. To outmaneuver the heinous plans of Hitler, the US were allied with the Britain to defeat Germany. With the arrival of General Eisenhower in London, Britain was poised to wage a great war to free the world from the tyranny of the German assaults. Vilayat and his crew were docked on the beaches of Normandy to deliver men, weapons, and equipment to the allied forces. If Noor's absence was not enough to crush Pirani's heart with grief, Vilayat's mission for clearing a safe passage for thousands of vessels that were to cross the channel waters in the dead of the night until the break of dawn, was pounding her very soul to bleeding lumps.

Pirani's nightmares, without fail, were reenacting the war scenes, which she could watch shifting rapidly. At times she could see herself standing at the harbor in Normandy, witnessing in horror thousands of soldiers, dead or wounded, the sky above black with allied planes, slicing the very heart of the winds to reach somewhere, to drop bombs or paratroopers. This morning, still immersed in hoary nightmares, swiftly and astonishingly, Pirani was transported somewhere in Paris. The sky was overcast and a light drizzle on her hot cheeks was lending her comfort. Though her thoughts were fiery and through the ears of her heart she could hear Noor's voice ripping through the wind and the rain. *Mother, Mother, I want to be with you.* Pirani was jolted out of this nightmare to a rude awakening, sitting there shivering in the dark. She was hugging her knees and weeping as she had not wept before in years after Daya's death.

It was close to dawn, so Pirani heaved herself up with earnest effort, bathed and got ready for work. Recalling with another pang of agony that Vilayat must still be working or ready to snatch a few hours of rest before starting his second shift. He had written in detail how America and Britain were preparing to free France and to defeat both Japan and Germany. Trying to deflect her thoughts from the flood of pain and misery, she could see through her mind's eye the cunning ploy which Britain had erected to defeat the forces of Germany.

Thousands of dummy tanks, airplanes and landing craft were manufactured, either of wood and canvas, or of inflatable rubber. Such contraptions were to be placed all over the region of Kent in England to make it appear to the Germans that the obvious landing point in France would be at the Pas-de-Calais. Hope was that the Germans seeing this real-looking large-scale task force accruing in one place would be duped into concentrating their defenses in the Calais region.

In bewilderment, Pirani kept working and living the nightmarish reality with unending strain. Waves upon waves of young Americans were coming daily to England to free France under some grand scheme called the Operation Bolero. A makeshift artificial harbor was being created with enormous barges made of concrete, towed across the channel along with the floating bridge elements, to create a port comparable to that of Dover.

For Pirani, months were sliding past. Her birthday came and was gone without one scrap of a poem from Noor. She couldn't even see Claire on her birthday, and Vilayat's birthday in the same month went unacknowledged and uncelebrated. A month later was Hidayat's birthday and she didn't even know where he was living.

Suddenly, after nine months of occupation in France, Gestapo were moving out of the Avenue Fotch in France, sending a wave of relief in Britain that soon this ugly war would be the cold horror in the books of history. Only a fraction of relief came Pirani's way with the hope that Noor would be home soon. She heard on the news that Charles de Gaulle was heading a parade from the Arc de Triomphe to the Notre Dame. But her agony was doubled when she realized she didn't know where her daughter was?

Claire could now spare some time to visit Pirani now and then, but in finding out whereabouts of Noor, she felt helpless. Vilayat could snatch some time out of his working schedule and visit his mother, trying his best to console her with hopes, but like Claire feeling helpless, his own heart remaining inconsolable. A few months after Germany's retreat from France, the war in Europe was fizzling out, yet fear and unrest were ever present. Vilayat was even able to spare some time to visit Fazal Manzil, noticing that Nekbakht had found some furniture and personal belongings of their family and had transported those items to her house for safekeeping. From France he wrote to his mother.

Dear Amma,

The war is speeding towards a hasty conclusion today, and as you hear over the news broadcasts, camp after camp are being rescued and prisoners retrieved. So it is now just a question of time and this, judging from the general situation, it is going to be a short war now. Another month or two should see Germany in full retreat and overrun. Besides, the names of people released are not given for obvious reasons and there is always quite some delay in their coming back. For all we know, it is not impossible that Noor should even be making her way back just now. So just have moment's more of patience. Also, a rumor that Hitler has killed himself with a gun, his wife Eva committing suicide by taking cyanide.

While Pirani's patience was running out, her anxiety was ballooning. One month and a half after Vilayat's letter, she heard on the radio the unconditional surrender of Germany and the end of World War II May 8, 1945, the same day as her birthday and no word from Noor. No more needed at the hospital, she had started working afternoons and evenings collecting tickets at the cinema. Claire, too, no longer in active duty in the Army and without a payroll had found work in an old government office near the Victoria Station. She was earning a meagre salary by typing numbers on blue stencil paper. Still no news of Noor, though it was three months after Germany had left France and the victory was declared. Hitler's forces were completely routed from all quarters of Europe, though Japan continued to fight. Vilayat was to remain in the Commission with the Navy for another nine months, posted wherever he was needed, mainly in India, France or Holland. From Copenhagen he wrote.

Dear Amma,

Of course, it is terribly worrying. Time is flying by. Surely there must be some information available by now. I can never keep my mind off the subject, and it is becoming unbearable. I am writing to the War Office to ask whether we might not at this stage put in for news through the Red Cross. I am afraid I do not anticipate returning to England for quite a long time. I can tell you now, we are in Copenhagen. It is a wonderful city. I spend most of my time in the university library of psychology.

For Pirani, time had become an illusion, dark, static and bottomless. Her only comfort was Claire, both trying to console each other and both falling into the darkest pit of misery. More tears were added to Pirani's wretched plight when the news came that America bombed Hiroshima in Japan, killing thousands, the same day as Hidayat's twenty-eighth birthday. Three days later another devastating news that America bombed Nagasaki, killing thousands again, and the surrender of Japan. A few days later she received a letter from Vilayat who was in France and consumed with worry about Noor.

Dearest Mother,

The absence of news is enough to make one go mad, but I have been to quite a few organizations to discover that there are still thousands of prisoners of war—particularly French—mainly in the Russian zone and a lot of work is still being done sorting them. Till soon, love, Vilayat
PS: Noor would surely be sad to hear that Subhas Bose died in air crash.

A few weeks later, Pirani also received a letter from Hidayat, he was writing from Dieuleft, France.

Dear Mother,

I have not been able to write to you since so many years owing to the circumstances. During the first four years of German occupation, the correspondence with England was prohibited. Moreover, I was not able to correspond by means of Red Cross owning to the difficulties which would eventually arise on account of my British nationality. During the year which preceded Liberation, I was obliged to hide in the mountains with my wife and children. Now we have a girl named Inayat and besides Fazal, his younger brother Gayan. But I suppose Vilayat has told you about this. He came to us a month ago and gave me frightful news about Noor in not finding her whereabouts. Yours most affectionately, Hidayat.

Nothing could cauterize Pirani's heart of terrible pain in not knowing where Noor was, not even the news of her sweet grandchildren. Though she was grateful that Hidayat named her daughter after his father's last name. He had already named one son after Fazal Manzil in memory of Fazal Mai and now the other one he named Gayan, meaning spiritual knowledge as taught by Hazrat Inayat Khan.

Overwhelmed with anxiety, Pirani didn't have any strength to respond to any of her children, Claire trying her best to cheer her mother with rosary of hopes and prayers. One whole month scudded past since Hidayat's letter, and now she received another one from Ekbal Dawlat, the mother of Mahboob's wife Shadi, from Holland. Obviously Vilayat must have visited his uncle's family, now that he was posted in Holland.

My dear Begum,

For many, many years we did not hear from each other, but this does not mean, that my thoughts of sympathy and affection did not go very often to you and your children. We were so happy to see Vilayat and to see him in good health after these terrible years of war and devastation. Surely he will have told you that we also suffered much from the war. Cold, hunger, evacuation, bombardment on our house here and seven weeks of continual danger. But all is nothing in comparison with the agony you are going through about your heroine daughter, our Babuli. I can't tell you how much we all are longing to hear good news about Noor, hope is always there. Mahboob had a good dream about her, also Shadi saw her once in a dream. Many have yet not come back. Murshid and your eldest daughter had shown bravery and sacrifice which hardly any other person will show. With affection as always.

Your Ekbal

No prayers had touched Pirani's lips since France was liberated. Her heart and soul were caught in pincers of agony, longing to escape into realms distant where her beloved daughter was lodged undiscovered. Two months later after Ekbal's letter, to Pirani's great astonishment she received a letter from Vilayat who was posted in Chenbur some eighty miles from Bombay in India.

Dearest Mother,

I am studying like hell to get a degree in B.SC in the discipline of physiology. They say if you help yourself, God, too, comes in to lend a hand. Do not worry about a job, but to keep yourself busy. If you feel so inclined, why not do something voluntary? Or take a course in something that might prove useful. Dearest, I have been better off than I have ever been. And having paid off all my debts and being decently dressed at last, I do not anticipate putting in for any extensive expenses in the future. In fact, I could easily support you entirely. So please do not worry on that issue, we have enough to worry without this. I have written to the War Office, insisting again on some news whatsoever, at least more details of the situation. It is so trying.

Pirani had at least begun to realize how Vilayat and her other children were suffering, but she could neither appease her own agony, nor console their living torment.

A month later Hidayat sent a brief telegram.

Arrived Suresnes. House partial occupation Red Cross.

This brief note had stabbed Pirani's heart with the knife of despair, ripping open memories of love, grief and separation in the smoldering ashes of Fazal Manzil. Her very breath was caught in a litany of supplications, Daya, Noor, Daya, Noor, both absent, both dearly beloved.

Four more months of blind agony and Pirani could neither believe nor understand how a human being with such excruciating pain could still breathe to endure more living torment. Her pain was great indeed and ironically, she didn't know that she was yet to experience the full measure of torment and live to suffer most terrible of agonies endured only by the saints and the prophets. Vilayat had just returned from Srinagar in Kashmir, after communing with the sages in search of peace and understanding. Peace was nowhere and understanding would elude him for years, he didn't know either just like his mother.

***

The New Year already on its rungs of spring had brought Vilayat the ultimate blow of grief, so sudden and brutal that he reeled against its merciless assault. The War Office had sent him a letter and its sanitized announcement hit him with the force of a hurricane.

Your Sister, a squadron officer N. Inayat Khan died at the Natzweiler Concentration Camp on July 6, 1944. Your sister was arrested near Paris in October 1943 and remained in various prisons in and near Paris until May 1944. On May 12, 1944 a convoy of women left Fresnes Prison near Paris, and in the convoy were eight English girls, who were taken straight to Karlsruhe where they were put in a city jail for women. They remained there until the night of July 5, 1944 when four were taken to Natzweiler, your sister being the one among them.

Our representative have seen the two German women who were in charge of the jail at that time, as well as several former inmates of the prison, and she believes while the conditions were harsh, they were not intolerable, as was the case in some of the Concentration camps.

From a male German political prisoner at Karlsruhe who was employed on various tasks, we have heard the girls were collected between 4:00 or 5:00 AM in a large grey car in which were members of the S.S and the Gestapo. The girls arrived at Natzweiler between 1:00 and 3:00 PM on July 6, 1944 and were seen walking down the main Camp Street. Next morning, the inmates made inquiries and heard that the girls had received lethal injections and had been cremated.

I hope that the knowledge of this invaluable contribution that your sister made toward final victory in preparing the ground for the freedom of France, will comfort you in your great loss.

All who came in contact with her during the time of her imprisonment have spoken most highly of her morals and courage.

When ashen-faced Vilayat came home to tell Pirani and Claire that Noor was dead, Claire simply began to cry silently and noiselessly. In contrast, Pirani just stared ahead in a daze as if oblivious to the presence of Claire or Vilayat. Then she drifted toward her room, and sat down on her bed, dry-eyed, stunned. Suddenly, the knives of agony, much sharper than when her Daya had died, were stabbing her heart. Noor, Noor, the naked torment in her very soul was hugging the visage of her Babsy, but that visage was not to be arrested. The living, breathing pain in her heart and soul was raising bootless cries to the heavens, not daring to seek even crumbs of consolation. From the pincers of this stark grief and shock she would never escape, her wounded heart itself was witness to her anguished hopelessness.

Pirani's spirit was crushed, her health failing, but she continued to work to keep herself busy, hugging the memory of Noor within her breast like a beautiful wound not ever to be healed. Claire was always there to help and comfort her mother and Vilayat.

Vilayat, after the initial shock and grief, had let his agonized cries rip through the sky during the silence of the sleepless nights. He had vowed to himself that he would find the truth and bring the perpetrators of his sister's death to light and to make them pay for their crimes, receiving just punishments. Most heartrending to him was his mother's silent grief as she continued to drift into state of oblivion and listlessness. Devising means to appease her grief, he contacted Noor's Army Supervisor Vera Adkins, requesting her to talk to his mother about Noor's work, which might bring her some consolation.

Vera Adkins was very sympathetic and came to their house, hoping she could bring little comfort to the grieving mother. Pirani listened to Vera Adkins politely, but remained listless, only her heart weeping. Claire couldn't tell if her mother really paid attention to what Vera Adkins was saying.

Noor went to France in June 1943 as a wireless operator for a British officer who was working with the Resistance Movement in Paris Area. Noor had been very keen to work for the freedom of France. The one thing that worried her at the time of her departure was the fact, Mrs. Inayat, that you might remain without news of her, and she particularly asked that we should continue to write to you even if we did lose touch with her. Unfortunately, after months of magnificent work she was captured. It was only in the late spring of 1944 that we became aware of this, but in view of her special request and the imminent invasion, we continued our letters to you. We hoped that we might find her in France after the Liberation. After her imprisonment, Noor had managed one gallant attempt at escape which proved unsuccessful. She had even excited the admiration of her German captors, and she was not ill-treated.

Vilayat, though in perpetual mourning for the loss of his beloved sister, tried his best to comfort his mother, but Pirani's health was rapidly declining. She didn't say much and never talked about Noor. Even when Hidayat wrote from France and Vilayat read that letter to his mother that Noor was posthumously awarded the highest civilian reward, the Croix de Guerre with Gold Star, Pirani's gaze remained vacant, though she kissed both Claire and Vilayat before she said goodnight.

Weeks later, Pirani could muster enough courage to read Hidayat's note which he had sent along with the letter, about the citation when Noor was posthumously awarded the Croix de Guerre. It stated:

On the proposition of the Minister of the Armies, the President of the Provincial Government of the Republic, Chief of the Armies, Minister of National Defense, cites to the Order of the Army Corps.

A/S 10 Nora Inayat Khan WAAF sent into France by Lysander on June 16, 1943 as a wireless operator with the mission of assuring transmission between London and an Organization of the Resistance in the Paris Area. Shortly after her arrival a series of arrests broke up the Organization. Obliged to flee, she nevertheless continued to fulfil her mission under the most difficult of conditions. Falling into an ambush at Grignon in July 1943, her comrades and she managed to escape after having killed or wounded the Germans who were trying to stop them. She was finally arrested in October 1943, and deported to Germany.

This citation carries the award of the Croix de Guerre with Gold Star.

Signed by General Charles de Gaulle

The rivers of hot tears were churning a storm behind the blue gates of Pirani's eyes, but she couldn't stop reading the addendum with false hope of being close to her beloved daughter.

At the memorial service in Paris for Noor, Madame de Gaulle-Anthonioz, the general's niece and President of Association Nationale des Anciennes Deportees et Internees de la Resistance said:

Nothing, neither her nationality, nor the tradition of her family, none of these obliged her to take her position in the war. However, she chose it. It is our fight that she chose, that she pursued with an admirable and invincible courage.

No, we will never forget Noor Inayat Khan, auxiliary officer of the English Army who was also a fighter of the French Liberation Forces. She returned to France, gave up her marriage, left her training to replace the lives of ours that the Gestapo had decimated. She never gave up the fight, struggling up till the end against all natural prudence till her arrest. For all of us, for the children of our country, what a marvelous example!

Seated on her bed, shriveled with pain, Pirani's pale cheeks were bathed with tears hot and scalding. The rivers of agony which she had dammed up within her for so long was now a stinging deluge from which she didn't wish escape lest her lacerated faith in loving God be shattered to smithereens.

Noor, Baby, Babsy, Babuli, a cry of agony was ripped from the very wound in her soul, enveloping her in the pain comfort of half awareness, half oblivion. Her very lips were weaving this poem on the tapestry of her wounded heart.

O Lord of justice, these frail lips with iron, seal
Pray let me not speak, nay let me not reveal
Lest the fury of the gods burst in a hurricane
That lifteth me up from this earthly blame and gain

1947-1949 ~ Liberated From Life

O death my comforter art thou
The healer of my wounds enow
Thy yielding glance do I beseech
And for thy soothing hand I reach
I yearn for thee, years pass me by
Thou comest not, but from my cry
I hear an echo over the hill
A sacred duty first fulfil
~Pirani

India was already free from the yolk of the Britain, giving birth to bloody twins, India and Pakistan, Pirani was to learn much later. Her sacred duty, she knew, was to take care of her children, but her health was failing, and she could barely keep her grief ensconced. Though she had managed admirably since Vilayat started working as an Attaché of the Pakistan Delegation to the United Nations Assembly. That's when she learned about the Great Partition, also learning that Vilayat employed Claire as his secretary.

They all moved to a nice flat in London and Pirani helped shop for clothes for Claire and Vilayat. London was abuzz with the post partition news of India and Pakistan, its aftermath as horrifying as death and devastation during the World War II. Pirani bought several newspapers every day, devouring their contents, as if searching for the beloved soul of her husband in that war-torn continent of blood and brutalities. But Claire, with her keen perception, knew that her mother was searching for more news of Noor in the newspapers. Somehow, she also knew that Vilayat knew more about Noor's work and disappearance, but he didn't want to share it with her or with his mother.

Rightfully so, for he knew that any knowledge of Noor's struggles would make his mother ill and distraught. He himself was consumed with anguish and bitterness, wanting to know more about the tragic events and to bring the murderers to the court for just punishments. The details he discovered were heartrending, but he kept them to himself, sharing only a few with Claire. He had become as sensitive as Noor, trying forever to shield his mother from exposure to any tragic news, but forgot to inform the War Office not to send any information about Noor to his mother. One evening as he returned home from work, he found his mother gasping for breath and suffering sharp pangs of discomfort in the very pit of her stomach. Claire told him that their mother just received a letter from the War Office. It stated that the officials of Natzweiler Concentration Camp were to be tried as war criminals at the Wippertal. Helping his mother to regain composure, Vilayat was crushed under the burden of his own guilt and chagrin in neglecting to warn the War Office against sending any letters to his mother.

It took weeks before Pirani could regain her strength. She thought it was a miracle, but she knew she was rediscovering the nectar of inspiration in poesy to mitigate her grief.

O Beloved I shudder and I shrink
Dare I to speak, ah, dare I once to think
Of ever again that only longed for bliss
To fall upon the dust, thy feet to kiss
Dare I to weep, my tears would form a sea
And in that sea, I would drown in ecstasy
O, Beloved, dare I to ask to die
This soul released, instantly to thee wouldst fly

Meanwhile, Vilayat had instructed the War Office not ever to send any letters to his mother, for any mention of Noor or of concentration camps made her very ill on the brink of expiring. He himself was finding quite a jamboree of conflicting details about Noor's agonized days of captivity in the concentration camp. His anguish was doubled by the latest reports and a chance encounter with a Dutch prisoner by the name of Joop who had been in the same concentration camp where Noor was taken. Joop told Vilayat about Wilheim Ruppert, the assistant camp director who had tortured Noor. With this new ammunition of horrors, making him livid with rage, Vilayat literally ran to the War Office, screaming at the Officer in charge of the War Crimes.

"What is the truth about my sister, really? The jail-keeper who is said to have beaten my sister is still holding his post to this very day. I have learnt that she was undressed by a Nazi brute by the name of Ruppert and beaten most mercilessly. When she was all bloodied, he told her he would shoot her. She was ordered to kneel, but she did not cry or plead for mercy. The only word she uttered before Ruppert shot her from behind through the head was, liberte."

Vilayat had then started crying like a child when the Officer put his arms around his shoulders, saying, "Sir, we will bring the torturer to just punishment soon."

Anguish cutting through each fiber of his soul and spirit, Vilayat kept searching for truth about his sister's tragic death, but never telling a word to his mother. He was closely watching his mother recover slowly and steadily, and that was a great consolation to his heart broken and restless. While Pirani was gaining health, it suddenly dawned upon Vilayat that Claire was keeping her grief to herself and falling prey to depression. To lift her from this imminent pool of depression, he decided to share some of Noor's less painful conditions during her captivity. He also showed her the letter the War Office had sent to their personal staff in general after his angry outburst at the Officer of the War Crimes.

Mr. Vilayat Inayat Khan informed us that his mother is in a very precarious state of health, and in the opinion of her medical advisor any severe shock would be sufficient to cause her death. In view of this Mr. Vilayat Inayat Khan and his sister Claire have so far kept the details of Noor's death away from their mother. He informed us that he was seeking power of attorney which would enable him to deal with all his mother's affairs and particularly matters arising out of his sister's death. In order that his mother might be spared of any further worries, we suggest therefore that at any rate your preliminary approach to Mrs. Inayat Khan should be made through his son at the address given.

Pirani's health was improving, though she had lost weight and looked pale, rather ethereal. She was getting into the routine of going to the market every day and buying groceries and bringing home stacks of newspapers and scanning each line in hope of getting any more news about Noor. The little strength which she gathered each day was the soma of her inspiration. She was missing Noor's birthday poems and her joyful bursts of poetry, but her own were reaching out to her Daya, daring not to tell him how Noor had suffered, looking for some salve to heal her own living torment.

Alone, alone at the early dawn
In springtime with its blossom wan
Thy glory do I gaze upon
And naught do I see but thee
Alone, alone, underneath shady trees
Midst summer warmth I feel thy breeze
Alas, I fall upon my knees
And naught I see but thee
Alone, alone through fallen leaves
That autumn scatters and interweaves
I trod the path, sweet memory grieve
And naught I see but thee
Alone, alone in the pure white snow
As the wintry winds around me blow
Firmly I stand, yet seeking to know
And naught I see but thee

***

The seasons had shifted and skipped without any news of Noor for Pirani. One entire year had slipped past and Noor was not there to send any birthday poems, nothing was left to celebrate. Life was more like a drill, Claire and Vilayat went to work, Pirani did her daily grocery shopping, and of course, newspapers. Suddenly, one day the War Office informed Vilayat that a commemorative report on Noor's heroic war story would appear soon in the British Newspapers. Vilayat felt devastated by this news, knowing that his mother would read this story and get ill again.

Vilayat was quick to take Claire into confidence, deciding that his sister and mother move to France immediately. That meant, Vilayat would still keep his job in London, but Claire would have to resign. With

Claire agreeing, Vilayat told his mother, now that France was liberated, it would be safe to live in Fazal Manzil and it would be more comfortable. Pirani didn't object, not even showing any sign of interest in knowing when they were leaving. She was drunk by the soma of her inspiration, as if inching her way closer to her eternal abode with her Beloved. Conscious of this abrupt move, when the darkness of the night descended, she poured out her grief in solitude.

Thou hast warned me of my duty
Which I can't forget
And thou sayest if I listen
I shall not regret
For duty's sake hence I am bound
To this world of grief
And never until I go to thee
Shall I find relief
Thou didst say when duty is done
I may follow thee
What a blessing, O Beloved
When thou callest me

Suresnes, the homeland of love and loss, of joys and sorrows, finally Pirani had returned home as a ghost of the ages past in search of her loved ones lost in Nether land. Returning to Fazl Manzil was like entering a shrine of memories, choking Pirani's heart to tears of blood, but her eyes didn't shed one single tear, instead she felt grateful even to tread the soil of France. Fazal Manzil was home, she could even envision the holy feet of her Daya treading softly in the garden. His music pouring sweetness into her heart. Claire took charge of the household duties to make sure that her mother was comfortable. Soon Hidayat and his family came for a visit. Pirani held her younger son close to her heart and his wife too, so very adorable. She couldn't stop hugging and kissing her grandchildren. Squeezing Inayat into her arms, her heart went somersaulting as if Daya's sweet breath was infused in every pore of this little girl, her own dear, dear grandchild. Her grandsons Fazal and Gayan were swept into her loving arms, too, and she could feel the scent of momentary bliss she had not felt in years. Later when she retired to her bedroom, alone and forlorn, she could feel the spiritual breath of Daya comforting her aching heart. She was writing feverishly, knowing not where her thoughts were coming from in such a torrent of downpour.

O Gayan, thou my treasured gem
I bow to thy command
Thou art the highest apothegm
Ever found on sea or land
Thou, inspiration, dost bestow
And deep, thy melody
A haunting sweetness dost thou show
With thy pathetic plea

Suresnes was on the mend after the war, but Pirani could see and feel the pulse of devastation, even at her own home at Fazal Manzil. Most of the precious pieces of furniture which Daya had purchased so lovingly were missing. The garden was in utter ruin, Claire wanted to help restore it to some semblance of order, but to Pirani such a task was daunting. After a few days of false sense of euphoria, Pirani was lost in the fogs of bitter memories. She didn't have strength even to shop for daily necessities. The freshly buried wound of Noor's death within her was gaped open once again after Hidayat and his family left Suresness. Fortunately, their old friends Sirkar and Saida Van Tuyll invited them to Holland for a vacation. Vilayat was still working in England, but hearing about this invitation from Claire, he urged her to take their mother to Holland without him, for it would be good for her health. Once again Pirani didn't object or question, disillusioned somehow that Noor would soon come to Fazal Manzil. Before leaving for Holland, she wrote another poem.

O loving friends, judge not my solitude
Nor my silence ye not comprehend
Forever are my loving thoughts bestrewed
Upon ye all with gratitude distend
But hark! My pain no remedy amends
This little spark of life, to him hath flown

Then what is left of me to greet my friends
Naught but deadened skin and withered bone
Forever in spirit shall I dwell
Amongst ye all, my loving friends of yore
But body, heart and soul doth bid farewell
Offering ye, these precious Rubies Four

Pirani and Claire stayed in Holland for two whole weeks. Their friends lodged them in a nice apartment in Hague so that they can rest in privacy and recover from the trauma of their loss. Claire was the strong one, always taking care of her mother, and Pirani's health improved as prophesied by Vilayat. After returning to Fazal Manzil, an old mureed of the Murshid, Baroness Farinola-de-Tanfani titled as Zebunisa invited them for a vacation in Italy and Switzerland. Pirani, this time, didn't want to go, but urged Claire to accept the invitation. Claire agreed reluctantly after extracting promise from her mother that in her absence she would take good care of her health. After Claire left, Pirani tried to bandage her bleeding heart with memories sweet and nostalgic. Besides writing new poems, she arranged her old ones in a book format. To escape the ruins of her own garden at Fazal Manzil, she sought the rose garden in her Daya's heart in sweet remembrance.

In an eastern rose garden full in bloom
Privileged be the few that walketh there
But to pluck the roses of sweet perfume
Is, from the heavens, an answered prayer
O ye blinded souls seeking earthly gain
A moment that lasteth and from ye flee
Go to that garden in quest—and obtain
The one Divine gain of eternity

Vilayat visited his mother on and off during Claire's vacation in Italy and Switzerland and found more time to visit after Claire returned from her vacations. Pirani still looked frail and rather restless. Some of the old Sufi friends had returned to Suresnes and were trying their very best to fulfil all the needs of their Murshid's family and to keep his wife comfortable. They were also picking up the broken pieces of the Sufi Movement and to let it regroup and flourish. Vilayat was already helping to accomplish just that, and in between his trips from England to France, another year was dissolved into oblivion. Four months into the New Year and Vilayat was informed that the British government was awarding posthumous award of George Cross to Noor. He wrote to Claire to bring their mother to London, so that they all could be together to receive this posthumous award. Pirani declined, telling Claire that she didn't want to go through another painful awakening in memory of her beloved daughter. Claire left alone, honoring her mother's decision as some talisman to help her through this saddest ceremony she was to witness along with her brother. As soon as Claire left, Pirani poured out her pain in one final outburst of inspiration.

Where art thou, O where art thou
Guiding light of my world
Dark shadows cross life's path
And by cruel winds I am hurled
In deepest seas I searched thee
I roamed to lands unknown
I soared the highest heavens
But still, bereft and lone
And when all hope had vanished
And no heed to my cries
It was then, thy light was shining
Form mine own dim eyes

Claire, concealing her own pain and sadness, had reached London to join Vilayat, both attending the award ceremony together and thinking about their mother. The King of England, George V1, personally handed the George Cross to Claire and Vilayat in memory of Noor. This decoration was awarded "for acts of greatest heroism or of the most conspicuous courage in circumstances of extreme danger" and was awarded to only three women, one of whom was Noor.

The King's official note from the Buckingham Palace read:

The Queen and I offer our heartfelt sympathy in your great sorrow. We pray that the Empire's gratitude for a life so nobly given in its service may bring you some measure of consolation.
Signed by George R. I

Meanwhile, back at Fazal Manzil, Pirani was wading through the waters of depression, at times caught in waves of inspiration.

Over the hills and dales and mountain peak
And over the seas, for him I would seek
If only I had wings
Then upward through the turquoise sky
Till the gates of paradise espy
There through all wonders would I fly
If only I had wings
The heavens far beyond I would soar
Seeking the one whom I adore
If only I had wings

Claire was still in London and Pirani was astonished, rather baffled to receive a letter from her old friend, Madame Peineau. She wrote warmly, sending her heartfelt condolences. Also writing that Noor was with her when Noor received Pirani's letter and a tin of sardines. Noor was so delighted, reading your letter over and over again. And she couldn't bring herself to eat the sardines as she regarded them too precious to be sent by her dear Amma.

After reading this letter from her old friend, Pirani cried her heart out, condoning the sudden spasms of pain in her stomach. She was aghast with grief and disbelief that she still had tears left after pouring them out in torrents for years. For the first time after her return to Fazal Manzil, she stumbled into Noor's room, hugging her daughter's harp which was recently returned to Fazal Manzil. Against the mist of tears stinging her eyes, she drifted to her bedroom, her very fingers burning with the flames of inspiration.

O beautiful face
Beaming with light
Whither hath it gone
How far its flight
Never to return to
This grinding life
Where there is naught but
Sorrow and strife

Exhausted with grief and enveloped in a mist of unshed tears Pirani had drifted into the comforting arms of sleep. Next day, the level of her pain in the stomach was high and she barely dragged herself out of her bed. Claire was to arrive late in the afternoon, so she took a leisurely bath which made her feel better. Close to noon, she was astonished once again by the surprise visit of her old family physician friend Dr. Pierre Jordan along with his wife. They had come to offer their condolences for the untimely death of Noor. Pirani served them tea and biscuits and they told her that they believed they were the last family to see Noor prior to her disappearance. The afternoon melted away in remembrance of Noor and as soon as the friends left, Pirani felt nauseated by sudden spasms of pain in her stomach. That's how Claire found her when she returned to Fazal Manzil. Frightened by her mother's painful condition, Claire wanted to take her to the hospital, but Pirani wouldn't allow.

"No, I will be fine, just bring me a cup of hot tea." Pirani managed to murmur, her pain abating a little. "But if I die, make sure I am cremated."

Claire began to weep silently, but Pirani ignoring her own pain, held out her arms. "Sorry, darling, I will be fine. Just fetch me a cup of tea."

Once in the kitchen, Claire called Vilayat to hurry home without delay. Back in the living room where Claire had found her mother, she didn't tell her that she called Vilayat. Pirani sipped her tea and wouldn't allow Claire even to call a doctor. After drinking her tea, Pirani wanted to go to her bedroom and Claire followed. Pirani sank into the comfort of her bed, while Claire hovered over her. Her mother looked comfortable and she didn't want to leave till she fell asleep, but Pirani insisted that she wanted to be alone and resting, assuring Claire that she was much better.

196

Claire lingered a while, kissed her mother and then went down to the living room. In the evening Vilayat called to let her know that he couldn't get the last flight from London, so he would reach Suresnes early in the morning. He sounded worried, but told Claire not to worry, saying that mother would be fine and that he would see them both in the morning.

Alone in her bedroom, Pirani sought the fiery torch of her inspiration and scribbled.

Hark! I hear my Beloved's call
It is piercing through my ears
Take me up to thy land of all
From life's long grieving years
Precious Rubies born of our love
Weep not, sorrow is past
Allah is with us both above
Happy we are at last
All parents must depart one day
Children, your lives begin
Love your mates, by happy and gay
Your father's message reign

Next morning when Vilayat came, he could not be deceived that his mother was suffering intolerable pain, so both Claire and Vilayat rushed her to the hospital. After examining her, the doctor decided that she was to be operated immediately for intestinal occlusion. Pirani kept insisting that she would be fine, but one look at the attending nurse who was a nun dressed in black, she could barely stifle her scream. Immediately she was taken to the surgical section of the hospital. Pirani had no time to recover from the surgery, for right on the operating table she passed away, seemingly against the intolerable surge of pain and horror.

***

May 1, 1949, the great American Queen, the mother of Rubies Four, was joined with her Indian Mystic in eastern skies, beyond pain and worldly struggles. It seemed she had bid farewell to the world days before she died. Claire found a new quatrain in her room. There was a note attached to that, intending to use this quatrain as a preface to her book of poetry.

Happiness be with our little ones
Right guidance from Above
I wish good luck in the home
And my deepest love

Noor, Claire, Murshid, Hidayat, Ameena Begum, Vilayat (front row);
Maheboob and Musharaff (rear)

Epilogue

Land of wonder, land of dream
Noble and of high esteem
Land where chosen jewels gleam
Guarded by the God Supreme
Land of priceless ancient scroll
Land of my despairing soul
With thy love my grief condole
Unto life's eternal goal
~Pirani

Honoring Pirani's dying wish, her Rubies Three cremated her body. Pirani's ashes were stored in an urn and kept at the cemetery. Claire and Vilayat talked about going to America and burying her ashes in her own family graveyard. Vilayat used to visit the cemetery quite often, but one evening he discovered that his mother's urn was gone. Upon inquiry he discovered that the urns were kept for a certain fee on monthly basis. He was not told about that, but since the management didn't receive their monthly payment, they threw out the urn even without issuing a warning. Vilayat was heartbroken, but Claire always the practical one consoled him that their mother's ashes were free in the light and air to be blown away into the blue sky of the Great Lord's Palace.

Paradoxically, this incident proved to be a testament of Pirani's love for her husband and children, infused into the very air of France and inside Fazal Manzil, nourishing life inside the Sufi Movement in Suresnes.

Were Pirani to come back, she would have found great consolation in the fact that her beloved daughter, who had given her life to the cause of France and Britain, would be eternally lodged in Fazal Manzil and in England.

In England there was a memorial to the members of FANY—to which Noor belonged, at Runymede.

And yet it was fortunate that she would not return to this world, for Noor was interned in Germany. At the Dachau Concentration Camp

Memorial Site, apart from the memorial plaque in the crematorium there is write-up in the museum and a copy of the marble plaque that was placed in front of Fazal Manzil.

Each year, toward the end of April, the town of Suresnes honors the memory of Noor at a ceremony in front of the memorial plaque placed on the wall outside Fazal Manzil.

In the lower part of the Suresnes, near the Seine River, a square was named after Noor: Coues Madeleine—her code name.

In Valency, France a monument was erected in Year 1991 to SOE's French section heroes of World War II, among whom Noor was remembered. The ceremony was presided over by the England's Queen Mother, as well. Other memorials to Noor's memory include:

A plaque in front of the family home, Fazal Manzil

A plaque in Dachau Camps Crematorium

Noor's name is engraved at Blois. The ceremony was presided over by the British Queen Mother. A memorial placed in England in Year 1953

All these memorials reflect the great love of Ora Ray Baker, married to the most loving spiritual Mystic of the East, Hazrat Inayat Khan.

To him, she was his Sharda—the goddess. Amina Begum, the blessed mother of his Rubies Four. Pirani, the wife of Pir, in essence the Mistress of the Sufi Masters. The message of Sufism is still alive in Fazal Manzil at Suresnes. Hazrat Inayat Khan's Sufi message is flourishing globally in all continents of the world and in cyberspace in this century Twenty-One.

The inner life is a journey divine
Passing scenes of wondrous beauty
Where heavenly flowers and fruits outshine
Sustained by the light of unity
And whenever is reached the eternal goal
Closed are the lips from explaining
The pure upliftment of the heart and soul
Merged into love all-pervading
~Pirani

Bibliography

Unpublished works of Hazrat Inayat Khan by the kind permission of his grandson, Pir Zia

Inayat Khan, Hazrat. The Wisdom of Sufism. Element Books Limited. 2000

Inayat Khan, Hidayat. Memories of my Beloved Father and Mother. Ekstasis Editions. 2002

Bernard, Pierre. Encyclopedia of Occultism and Parapsychology. The Gale Group. 2001

Harper, Ray Claire & Harper, Ray David. We Rubies Four. Omega Publications, Inc. 2011

Basu, Shrabani. Spy Princess, The Life of Noor Inayat Khan. Omega Publications. 2007

Fuchslin, Puran. Rosary of Hundred Beads, Pirani Ameena Begum Ora Ray Baker. Edition Petama Project Zurich. Reprinted 2008

Inayat Khan, Hazrat. The Heart of Sufism. Shambhala. 1999

Inayat Khan, Hazrat. A Pearl in Wine. Omega Publications. 2001

Pir Vilayat, Inayat Khan. Awakening. Penguin Putnam, Inc. 2000

Hidayat, Inayat Khan. Sufi Teachings. Ekstatis Editions. 1994

Special acknowledgment:

All poems written by Noor, Pirani and Hazrat Inayat Khan are taken from the book, Rosary of Hundred Pearls.

Some letters exchanged between Sharda and Daya are taken from, We Rubies Four.

Most letters written by Noor, Pirani and Murshid are taken from The Spiritual Message of Hazrat Inayat Khan from Wahiduddin's Web online.

Also lectures and discourses from, The Complete works of Hazrat Inayat Khan, by the courtesy of the Nekbakht Foundation.

About the Author

Farzana Moon is a poet, historian and a playwright. Writes Sufi poetry, historical, biographical accounts of the Moghul emperors and plays based on stories from religion and folklore. Her published works in religion and spirituality are: *Irem of the Crimson Desert; Sufis and Mystics of the World; Prophet Muhammad: The First Sufi of Islam; No Islam But Islam; Sharia Exposed.* Published works in the sequels of the Moghul emperors are: *Babur, The First Moghul In India; The Moghul Exile; Divine Akbar and Holy India; The Moghul Hedonist: Glorious Taj and Beloved Immortal; The Moghul Saint of Insanity; Poet Emperor of the Last of the Moghuls: Bahadur Shah Zafar.* Another of her published book in history is about the partition of India and Pakistan, *Holocaust of the East.* Her play *Osama The Demented* had a staged reading in Stockholm. Another of her play, *Russian Roulette,* is being considered for production. Her latest published book is, Quran and Wisdom of Hazrat Inayat Khan. Currently she is working on a book of plays.